Nonfiction Writing Power

*Teaching Information Writing
with Intent and Purpose*

Adrienne Gear

Pembroke Publishers Limited

For the three I love the most—Richard, Spencer, and Oliver

© 2014 Pembroke Publishers
538 Hood Road
Markham, Ontario, Canada L3R 3K9
www.pembrokepublishers.com

Distributed in the U.S. by Stenhouse Publishers
480 Congress Street
Portland, ME 04101
www.stenhouse.com

We acknowledge the financial support of the Government of Canada through the Canada Book Fund (CBF) for our publishing activities.

We acknowledge the assistance of the Government of Ontario through the Ontario Media Development Corporation's Ontario Book Initiative.

Library and Archives Canada Cataloguing in Publication

Gear, Adrienne, author
    Nonfiction writing power / Adrienne Gear.

Includes bibliographical references and index.
Issued in print and electronic formats.
ISBN 978-1-55138-293-7 (pbk.).--ISBN 978-1-55138-859-5 (pdf)

    1. Composition (Language arts)--Study and teaching (Elementary). 2. Creative writing (Elementary education). 3. English language--Composition and exercises--Study and teaching (Elementary). I. Title.

LB1576.G426 2014   372.62'3044   C2013-907486-4
                                                C2013-907487-2

Editor: Kat Mototsune
Cover Design: John Zehethofer
Typesetting: Jay Tee Graphics Ltd.

Printed and bound in Canada
9 8 7 6 5 4

MIX
Paper from
responsible sources
FSC® C004071

Contents

Preface

It is hard to imagine that not even ten years ago Reading and Writing Power did not exist. It is hard to believe that I am beginning what would appear now to be the final entry in a series I never intended to write. But through my teaching and my desire to share my experiences, four books have emerged. A friend asked me a short while ago, "How do you actually write a book?" I'm sure different writers would answer that question differently; for me, the book begins in my head and evolves through lessons I teach, conversations I have, books I read, workshops I give, and ideas that sift through my thinking. I walk around with a book swirling around my head for up to a year, until I think my brain is going to burst, and then I start to write. It is a relief, to say the least, to finally get it out of my head and onto paper.

But looking back, it was never my intent to be published or to write books. I do consider myself a writer, yet my intent has always been to teach. To teach, I realize over the years, is also to learn. And what I've learned in my nearly 25 years of teaching is that I have only one simple goal: to move my students forward in their learning and to support them in the best way I can along the way. Best practice results in best learning. It's as simple and as challenging as that. Good teaching practice is hard work: it requires patience, persistence, inquiry, reflection, the courage to take risks, the ability to admit mistakes, and the desire to find new ways to make learning better for our students. It is about explicit and purposeful teaching, and not just assigning and assessing. It is about recognizing that the reason your students might not be doing very well is not so much about them as about you. It is about being willing to ask yourself, *Am I providing my students with what they need to move forward in their learning? And if not, what could I be doing do better?*

I, like many teachers in this ever-changing world of technological advancements, am overwhelmed by the numerous ways we are now able to weave technology into our teaching practice. The overhead projectors and Gestetner machines of the dark ages have been pushed aside for document cameras, tablets, interactive whiteboards, and other high-tech gadgets. Grade 1 students are now learning through blogging and tweeting. Teachers can access hundreds of teaching ideas in seconds with a click of a mouse. I am more than impressed (and a tad envious) when I see how many teachers have effortlessly woven their best teaching practice into this new technological era, while I still make my anchor charts on chart paper. But in some cases, I question whether the strong desire to have a tablet in the hands of every child is becoming more a focus than the lesson itself. I, like many teachers, have become hooked on online pinboards. Before I know it, an hour has passed while I sift through all the amazing teaching ideas. And while I get excited about seeing and trying some of these new ideas, I find myself also wondering how some of these isolated lessons might connect to the bigger picture. Yes, students are learning, but is there real purpose and intent behind the learning?

When I first started teaching, I admit it was these short, quick-fix, fill-the-afternoon-and-bulletin-board lessons I searched for. Sometimes, it was enough for me to get through a day! But now, my seasoned teaching spirit has become focused on one primary goal—to teach with purpose. Everything I teach my students needs fit into a bigger picture. And not only does that big picture need to be clear for me, it also needs to be made clear to my students. "Why am I teaching this to you?" "Why is it important for you to learn this?" These questions are the foundation of everything I teach. Intention and purpose: it somehow needs to fit.

Writing instruction should always come hand-in-hand with intent and purpose. While it might be relatively easy for a teacher to assign a topic for writing and provide a mini-lesson and a few instructions, are students fully aware of the purpose for the writing, the *why* behind the lesson? Are young writers aware of their reader when they are writing? Do they consider what they want their reader to understand from their writing? Nonfiction writing, in particular, is grounded in intent. Writers of information begin with a purpose: an intent to describe, instruct, persuade, compare, explain, or report something to their readers. And writer's intent brings me directly to the underlying foundation of Writing Power—the intimate relationship between reader and writer. *We write to invite thinking.* This is a phrase I commonly use when I'm teaching writing to my students. Before a writer begins writing, it is essential for him or her to understand the intent for the reader, what the writer wants the reader to gain, learn, or understand from the piece. Ultimately, this is the big picture of writing instruction, the *why-we-write* rather than the *what-to-write* and *how-to-write*. The construction of writing should ultimately be for our readers; in no other form of writing is this more relevant than nonfiction.

And so, my goal for this book—my intent in writing—is, of course, to provide teachers with the *how* and *what* of nonfiction writing. But beyond the scripted lessons, reproducibles, and recommended anchor books you will find here, my intent for you, my reader, is to help move you to a place in your writing instruction where writing with intent and purpose becomes the focus of every lesson you teach, so that the reader on the receiving end of every piece of writing your students do becomes as important as the writing itself.

Introduction

Linking Writing Power to Nonfiction

Writing Power is an approach to writing instruction that focuses on writing to engage and connect with the reader. "We write to invite thinking" is the foundation of this approach, with an intentional effort to address the close, intimate link between reader and writer. Writing Power

- integrates the research of Donald Graves (1983) that revealed what good writers do, including the stages of the writing process: plan, write, edit/revise, and share.
- explores the explicit teaching of the writing techniques, or traits (Spandel, 1990), that enhance the quality of writing, including using interesting details, interesting words, similes, personification, voice, and the senses.
- uses *anchor books* as models of writing style, writing techniques, and topics.

The lessons in my book *Writing Power* were designed around writing fiction—personal narratives and stories, with a brief look at poetry—but all focused on writing with the intent of engaging, connecting, and inviting the reader to think. The lessons in this book focus on writing nonfiction and explore different forms or structures of nonfiction writing, including description, instruction, persuasion, comparison, explanation, and reporting. But the purpose behind all the lessons is the same—writing with the reader in mind.

The underlying principles of Writing Power originated from my work in the area of reading comprehension. Because of the important shift in the last ten years toward more explicit instruction in reading comprehension strategies to enhance understanding, many students have become familiar with applying thinking strategies to the reading process. These thinking strategies, based on the research of David Pearson (1983) include making connections, visualizing, asking questions, inferring, and transforming (synthesizing). With Writing Power, I explored these strategies, but looked at them from the writer's perspective. As a writer, how can I write to invite a visual image? How can I write to invite my reader to make a connection? How can I write to invite my reader to infer? Through this shift in perspective from writer to reader, writing lessons have taken on a different focus. We are now learning to become better writers not for ourselves, or for a mark, but for our readers.

I knew, even before I had completed my Writing Power book, that it only made sense for me to follow it up with a companion book on nonfiction writing. As with my Reading Power books, my first Writing Power book focuses on writing fiction and my second, the one in your hands, on writing nonfiction.

The underlying principles of Writing Power are also the foundation for this book: we are learning to write and to improve our writing skills not for ourselves, but for our readers. All writers write because they have something they

My struggle with linking this book to *Writing Power* was figuring out how to best organize it around the same strategies. After a great deal of thought, I decided that I couldn't. Because nonfiction writing is specifically broken down into different forms, or structures, it makes more sense to organize this book around these forms.

want to share with someone else. Writers of fiction have stories to tell and experiences to share—some completely imaginary; some embedded in experiences. Fiction writers want to entertain their readers with humor, to romance them, to excite them with adventure, to tug on their heartstrings and make personal and emotional connections. Writers of nonfiction have information that they feel is important and interesting to share with their readers. Because of that desire to share with someone else something we know or have discovered, it is important that we write in a clear, interesting, and engaging way. We not only want our readers to finish reading what we write, but also want to engage them, connect to them, inform them, teach them, persuade them, instruct them, or stimulate their thinking. And in some circumstances, we might even inspire them, move them, and possibly transform their thinking or their actions in some way.

The principle of *writing for the reader* can be applied to both fiction and nonfiction writing instruction. In terms of nonfiction writing, this concept plays a key role in helping young writers understand the purpose of all forms of nonfiction. From blogging to tweeting to reporting to instructing—the world of social media is certainly encouraging writers think carefully about who might be on the receiving end of their words and how their words can be perceived. More than ever, our students need to learn the structure, purpose, and intent of a wide range of writing forms that will help them navigate successfully through the written world of essay writing, provincial and state exams, and university and job applications—not to mention blogging, texting, and tweeting. But is our classroom writing instruction really doing enough to help students learn the impact and power of their writing? Is our writing instruction reflective of the real-world writing that students encounter in their day-to-day lives?

Visualize an old-fashioned balancing scale. One side of the scale is labeled *Fiction*, and the other *Nonfiction*. Now take a moment to consider all the writing experiences you provide for your students in your classroom. What percentage would you say are fiction and what percentage nonfiction? Now think about reading. What about read-alouds? Reading groups? Your classroom library? Put it all together and consider how your scales would be sitting. Are they balanced 50/50? Or are they tipping more toward the fiction side? Toward the nonfiction side? Finally, think about the many reading and writing experiences you have in a single day, everything you read and write as an adult in the real world. How many of those would be considered fiction and how many would classify as nonfiction? Think about the newspaper articles, recipes, instructional manuals, signs, blogs, e-mails, texts, tweets, catalogues, application forms, letters, lists, pamphlets, want-ads, newsletters, and programs you might read in a single day. Now compare that to how many times you pick up a novel, picture book, or fairy tale. Truth be told, there appears to be a disconnect between the reading and writing experiences we are providing for our children in school and those we actually experience on a day-to-day basis.

When I first read Tony Stead's book *Is That a Fact?* more than 10 years ago, I was completely transformed. His book about nonfiction writing changed my thinking and my practice. In it, he states that teachers are actually limiting students' ability to effectively write nonfiction because we spend so much of our classroom time on teaching them to write fiction. Ten years ago, I was certainly guilty of focusing the majority of my literacy lessons on fiction, believing that my once-a-year trip to the library to teach my students how to research and write an animal report sufficiently covered nonfiction writing. Since that time, however, I have grown to appreciate how critical a component of a complete writing

"Fictional narrative will not be enough to help us through life's journey." — Tony Stead

"Children write personal narratives and stories not because this is the limit of their experiences but because they don't know how to write outside these forms." — Tony Stead

program nonfiction writing actually is. I have heeded Tony Stead's caution that nonfiction writing involves a lot more than writing reports about animals. I have also grown to understand the importance of the reader, purpose, form, and language in nonfiction writing.

So why do we often limit our students' nonfiction experiences to writing about what an animal looks like, where it lives, and what it eats? Perhaps some of us believe that younger children are not developmentally ready for more complex types of texts. But many of the experts in the field, including Lucy Calkins (1986), Donald Graves (1989), Tom Newkirk (1989), and Tony Stead (2002), would disagree completely with that theory; they tell us that young learners can be writing all different forms of nonfiction if they are given the right kind of immersion, demonstration, and engagement. I believe it has a lot to do with our comfort zone and knowledge base as teachers. I'm comfortable with the straightforward, descriptive animal report because I understand it and have had a lot of experience with it. Such is not the case with, for example, persuasion and comparison. As a result, my nonfiction writing program consisted of what I knew best: descriptive reports about animals. Over the last several years, I have been exploring other forms of nonfiction and have become more familiar with them. My hope is that this book will help you move out of your comfort zone, become more comfortable with different nonfiction writing forms, and begin to explore them with your students.

Connecting Reading Power to Writing

My first book, *Reading Power*, established Reading Power as an approach to comprehension instruction that focuses students' attention on their thinking and enables them to find meaning from text based on their own ideas, experiences, and background knowledge. This practical approach to reading comprehension has provided teachers with specific strategies to teach students to use while they read, shifting the focus of reading comprehension from *what to think* to *how to think*. The Reading Power strategies, based on David Pearson's research into what strategies proficient readers use when they read (Pearson & Gallagher, 1983) include making connections, visualizing, questioning, inferring, synthesizing (transforming), and determining importance. "Zooming in" to nonfiction text features is a strategy I included in *Nonfiction Reading Power*. Through this focus on the more-complex approach of thinking through a text rather than simply retelling it, students are taught specific strategies to use to enhance their understanding of what they are reading, as well as a language to articulate their thinking.

My transition into Writing Power came as a result of considering these reading strategies from a writer's perspective. After many years of telling students that good readers think while they read, I began to consider what made this thinking possible. Why do I make a connection to certain books but not others? Why am I able to visualize easily with this book but not that one? These questions led me realize that my thinking is often guided by the writing itself. The writing, one could argue, was *inviting* me to connect, to question, to visualize, to infer. When I make a connection to something I'm reading, it's not that I, as the reader, have made that connection happen; often it is the writer inviting me, through the writing, to make that connection. When I visualize, I would not be able to do so were it not for the writer's intention of creating a visual image with his or her words. This intimate link between the reader's thinking and the writer's intent became the foundation for my first Writing Power book, which focuses primarily on personal narratives and story writing.

We can see that there is a strong need for students to develop an understanding of the various forms of writing—forms beyond storytelling and report writing. Developing a book that supports the teaching of nonfiction writing was an important next step for me. And while the organization of this book differs slightly from the previous three, it is important to emphasize how it connects to all that has come before it. *Reading Power* and *Nonfiction Reading Power* promote the notion that, when we read, we need to think. *Writing Power* and *Nonfiction Writing Power* promote the notion that, when we write, we need to invite thinking. (There you have a summary of all four of my books!) The clear link between Reading Power and Writing Power is *thinking*. As a teacher, it is no longer enough for me to teach reading and writing as separate subjects; I need to guide students to recognize that these actions are intimately linked through the power of thinking. I can't imagine teaching a writing lesson now without discussing the importance of writing to engage and invite the reader to think. I can't imagine teaching a reading lesson now without emphasizing the importance of how the writing invites our thinking. Reading and writing are intimately linked through thinking.

As I considered how this book would be organized, I realized that the link to thinking would continue to be the foundation upon which I structure the lessons, even though the specific lessons are organized around the nonfiction writing forms rather than the thinking strategies. However, it is important that we continue, while teaching nonfiction writing, to emphasize to our students the notion of writing for the reader. Because different forms of nonfiction are used for different purposes, writers of nonfiction need to be very clear on intent for their reader. It is also interesting to consider how different forms of nonfiction writing can promote different thinking strategies. Below are some ways we can continue to provide our students with links to thinking of the different forms of nonfiction:

- **Descriptive writing** invites readers to visualize and determine importance.
- **Instructional writing** invites readers to visualize and sometimes to transform their actions.
- **Persuasive writing** invites readers to make connections and transform their thinking.
- **Comparison writing** invites readers to make connections, ask questions, and zoom in.
- **Explanation writing** invites readers to question and visualize.
- **Nonfiction Narrative** invites readers to make connections, question, visualize, infer, and determine importance.

The strategies of thinking are an essential component of writing instruction. Writing with intention and purpose is an essential component of nonfiction writing. In my attempt to incorporate both in the organization of this book, form won out over strategy. However, I encourage you to continue to use the language of thinking and to promote thinking strategies throughout these lessons.

What to Expect

This book is designed to help teachers develop a writing program that focuses on the different forms of nonfiction through writing with intent. It is also meant to help teachers begin to develop ways to link up their writing instruction to the content areas of science and social studies. As in all my books, my intention is to make things as practical and straightforward as possible by providing teachers with a book they can pick up and use. In this book, you will find outlines of specific lessons, along with reproducible organizers and anchor book suggestions to accompany the lessons.

The first chapter provides the background and explanation for nonfiction writing forms that teachers will need to understand before launching into specific lessons. I outline the specific text structures covered in this book: description, instruction, persuasion, comparison, explanation, and nonfiction narrative. I discuss the specific teaching elements for each structure and provide a detailed description of each: the purpose, text form, language, and links to content areas.

The next chapter outlines the components of Nonfiction Writing Power. Included in this section are explanations of the Nonfiction Writing Power lesson framework, a detailed breakdown of a weekly writing schedule (based on the writing process), as well as thoughts about conferencing and editing.

Chapter 3 introduces the "big picture" concepts connected to Nonfiction Writing Power, including nonfiction text structures, writer's intent, writer's goals, and writing techniques. Following an explanation of each of these concepts is a scripted lesson to help teachers introduce these important background ideas to their students. In particular, the section Nonfiction Writing Techniques provides teachers with lessons for introducing a wide variety of writing techniques that, once introduced, can be applied throughout the weekly writing lessons. These techniques include incorporating nonfiction text features, adding interesting details, using triple-scoop words, making comparisons, writing with voice, crafting great beginnings, and organization.

Finally, the chapters on the Nonfiction Writing Powers provide overviews of the Nonfiction Writing Power or form, including a list of anchor books and notes on intent, form, language features, writing techniques, and assessment. They go on to outline explicit and sequential writing lessons that focus on each of the six nonfiction text structures: description, instruction, persuasion, comparison, explanation, and nonfiction narrative. Each lesson, regardless of the form, supports the notion of writing with purpose and intent. Often, the first lesson in a chapter outlines a *whole-class write*, in which the teacher models the new structure with student participation. As always, each lesson is supported by recommended anchor books, and extensions to individual lessons and to the text structure are provided.

1 What Is Nonfiction Writing Power?

Nonfiction Writing Powers

The world of nonfiction writing is huge. In fact, when it comes right down to it, nonfiction writing is any form of writing that is not story writing. It is scientific writing, report writing, essay writing, persuasive writing, instructional writing, expository writing, descriptive writing, letter writing, e-mailing, blogging, texting, tweeting—the list goes on and on. Each writing form has a specific purpose, a unique structure, and particular language features associated with it. Most elementary teachers are familiar with descriptive writing and, while it is important to teach descriptive report writing, there are many other forms of nonfiction writing that students should be introduced to and have experience with in elementary grades. These nonfiction writing forms, or powers, are outlined in this book:

- Description
- Instruction
- Persuasion
- Comparison
- Explanation
- Nonfiction Narrative (biography, current and past events)

NONFICTION TEXT FORMS = POWERS

Form	Writer's Intent	Example
Description	To provide reader with facts and information about a topic	• Descriptive reports on countries, animals, plants, insects, etc. • Classroom blogs • Online book or movie reviews
Instruction	To provide reader with instructions on how to achieve a goal, do something, make something, get somewhere	• How something works: e.g., manuals, how to use something, how to fix something, survival guides • How to do or make something: e.g., recipes, rules for games, science experiments, crafts, instructions on starting a blog page • How to live (human behavior): e.g., how to succeed, be happy, be rich

Persuasion	To share an opinion with the reader or attempt to convince the reader to take an action of some kind	• Opinion piece: e.g., favorite book, movie, pet, season • Persuasive piece: e.g., you should eat a healthy diet; no school uniforms; best chocolate bar to buy; our school is the best • Classroom blogs or online reviews
Comparison	To share with the reader similarities and differences between two topics or ideas	Compare (similarities) and contrast (differences): e.g., rabbits and hares; Canada and Japan; cars then and now
Explanation	To provide reader with facts explaining how or why something happens	Scientific Explanations: e.g., how a spider spins a web, why some things float and some sink
Nonfiction Narrative	To provide reader with sequential description of events in a person's life, a current or a historical event	• Biography of famous or non-famous person • Autobiography • Current event/newspaper article • Past event • Blogs or tweets

Teaching the Powers: Scope and Sequence

I am not suggesting that teachers attempt to teach all six text forms in a single school year. Teaching these forms of writing takes time, and students need many opportunities to practice them with a wide range of topics. Exposing them to a new form of writing in one lesson and assigning one piece of writing isn't enough. Students need to be immersed and engaged in a particular writing form for several weeks or months. They need to be exposed to many examples of these forms through classroom book collections, anchor books, and daily read-alouds. Realistically, you might be able to focus on two or three nonfiction writing forms per school year. See page 19 for the Content-Area Connections chart, where teachers from a grade can list science and social studies topics and brainstorm ways that the nonfiction forms can be linked up to their units of study.

As a group, teachers have to work collaboratively to develop a plan of scope and sequence to ensure that all forms are being covered, with the goal of students having been introduced to and having had practice writing all six forms at least twice by the time they leave elementary school. The Nonfiction Writing Scope and Sequence template on page 20 is designed to help a whole school teaching staff designate different writing forms to different grade levels (see sample on page 16).

If a form of nonfiction writing that you enjoy teaching is not assigned to your grade, go ahead and teach it, as long as you are still covering the forms for which your grade is responsible.

Teachers at all grade levels can plan the teaching of nonfiction writing by enlarging the chart on page 20 and working collaboratively on the scope and sequence of the instruction.

Grade 2	Grade 4	Grade 7
Social Studies	**Social Studies**	**Social Studies**
• *Communities* • *Canada* • *Mapping* • *Nutrition*	• *Aboriginal People and culture – past and present* • *Early Settlers* • *Canadian Explorers*	• *Ancient Civilizations: Rome, Egypt, Greece, Mayans, China, India, Early Humans*
Science	**Science**	**Science**
• *Animal growth and change* • *Properties of matter* • *Air, Water, Soil*	• *Habitat and communities* • *Light and Sound* • *Weather*	• *Ecosystems* • *Chemistry* • *Earth's Crust* • *Diversity of Life*
Nonfiction Writing Powers PERSUASION • *Our school is the best school* • *_____ is the best province to visit* • *_____ is the best animal* • *Should animals be kept in zoos* INSTRUCTION • *Recipes for healthy snacks* • *How to be an _____ (people in the community)* • *Science experiment* • *How to take care of pet* DESCRIPTION • *Animal report (using text features)* EXPLANATION • *How matter changes (ice to water)*	**Nonfiction Writing Powers** PERSUASION • *Catalogue of aboriginal clothing* • *Compare and contrast habitats – which would you rather live in?* • *Who was the greatest explorer* EXPLANATION • *How clouds are formed* • *How the water cycle works* • *How sound travels* INSTRUCTION • *How to build a totem pole, button blanket* • *How to plan a potlatch* • *How to make an aboriginal shelter* BIOGRAPHY • *Canadian Explorers (Cartier, Champlain, etc.)*	**Nonfiction Writing Powers** INSTRUCTION • *How to Be… Handbooks: Roman gladiator/ Egyptian/Greek god/ early human* EXPLANATION • *Chemical reactions – how they occur* • *Earth plates shifting – how natural disasters occur* • *How ancient inventions worked* DESCRIPTION • *Different ecosystems* • *Day in the life of a micro-organism* COMPARISON • *2 different ecosystems*

Nonfiction Writing Power and Content Areas

Writing is a cross-curricluar skill, as is reading. We write in all subject areas in various forms: in science, we write experiments; in social studies, we might develop a timeline. It makes sense, then, to use these subject areas as springboards for writing. Once students have learned and had practice in the purpose, structure, and language features of each of the different writing forms, they can apply their knowledge to writing in the content areas. Different content areas lend themselves better to different forms, so the key is to try to link the specific topic you are teaching to the best writing form; see sample below.

Sample of Writing Ideas for a Content-Area Topic

Content area: Science

Topic: Weather

- **Description** – describe the weather in different seasons

- **Instruction** – how to make a snowman

- **Persuasion** – which weather is the most deadly to humans?

- **Explanation** – how do rainbows form?

- **Comparison** – compare hurricane with tornado

- **Nonfiction Narrative** – Hurricane Sandy report

Nonfiction Writing Features

Stories are familiar territory to most children. When reading a story, they come to expect the structure of a beginning, middle, and end. They come to anticipate that the character will face and overcome some sort of challenge, and can often predict the "happy ending" with which everything will be tied up neatly by the last page. Over years of sharing stories, young children also become familiar with the language associated with fictional narrative: "Once upon a time,"; "Suddenly…"; "One day,"; "And they lived happily ever after." When transitioning from teaching students in reading stories to instructing them in writing, teachers often refer to familiar structures and language to which children have already been exposed. With nonfiction writing, however, this transition is often not as smooth, because students might not be as familiar with the structures and language of nonfiction forms as they are with fiction. This unfamiliarity is caused by their limited exposure to the different forms, as well as by the fact that there are only two main structures of fictional narrative, compared to the numerous different forms of nonfiction.

One of the keys to success in nonfiction writing is your students' understanding of the specific features associated with each nonfiction form: its purpose or intent, its structure, and its language. Through this knowledge, they can begin to recognize and differentiate between the various nonfiction forms, and the world of nonfiction writing can truly open up for them. Regardless of which nonfiction writing form you are teaching, introducing your students to the specific intent, structure, and language of the form can ultimately be the key to their success in writing.

Intent

Purposeful writing results when the writer has a clear intent in what he or she wants to write, why he or she is writing, and—most importantly—who the reader is. Nonfiction writing has many purposes: to describe, to instruct, to explain, to persuade or convince. It is essential for a writer of nonfiction to establish purpose and intent for the reader before beginning to write. Teaching students the purpose of each form of nonfiction is the key to linking reader and writer. Recognizing and establishing intent before writing can make a huge difference, not only for the writer, but also for the reader, who is led to a clearer and more engaging experience.

Structure

Katie McCormack, my friend and a teacher in Kamloops, BC, once told me that teaching text structure to her students was like handing over the keys to the car: without the keys, you can't leave the garage, but once the keys are in your hand, you're off and running!

Text structure refers to the "inner skeleton" of a piece of writing. During the 1970s and '80s, a great deal of research went into the examining text structures. Meyer (1975, 1981) was one of the first researchers to classify expository texts into different design structures, including cause–effect, compare–contrast, and problem–solution. In addition to writer's intent, a key to successful nonfiction writing is having a clear understanding of the structure of the specific form in which one is writing.

In my previous books, I included songs and chants as *hooks* to help my students understand certain concepts. To hook my students into different text structures, I have created word patterns for each (see chart below). These quick rhymes can be shared with students as new Nonfiction Powers (forms) are introduced. They are also used to help students plan their writing, as the key words from the rhyming patterns are reinforced in many of the planning pages.

Thanks to Barry Clarke, principal in Princeton, BC, for helping me create this chart!

WHAT THE STRUCTURES SAY

Descriptive writing says...	Instructional writing says...	Persuasive writing says...	Comparison writing says...	Explanation writing says...	Nonfiction Narrative says
What	What	What	Both	How/Why	Who/What
What	What	Why	Same	Because	Where
What	How	Why	Different	Because	When
What		Why	End	So there!	How
What		What was that again?			WOW!

Language

In *Teaching Text Structures*, Sue Dymock and Tom Nicholson refer to the specific language of writing forms as "the signal or cue words to highlight the structural organization of the text" (2007: 31).

If you ask a group of students what words or phrases they associate with story writing, many will likely identify common story language, such as "Once upon a time," "One day…," and "…happily ever after." But how many students would be able to identify key words and phrases associated with persuasive, instructional, or comparative writing? As mentioned, this disparity of familiarity is likely due to the greater exposure to the language of story children have in elementary school, compared with the language of the various nonfiction forms, which are largely unknown and untaught. Along with intent and structure, teaching students the specific key words and phrases associated with each nonfiction writing form is the third essential component to successful nonfiction writing. Lessons on introducing intent, structure, and language can be found in Chapter 3, and explicit lessons on each form can be found in the chapters on each of the six Nonfiction Writing Powers.

Content-Area Connections

Grade _____

Social Studies	
Science	
Nonfiction Writing Powers	Description: Instruction: Persuasion: Comparison Explanation: Nonfiction Narrative:

Nonfiction Writing Scope and Sequence

Kindergarten	Grade 1	Grade 2	Grade 3	Grade 4	Grade 5	Grade 6	Grade 7
Social Studies	Social Studies	Social Studies	Social Studies	Social Studies	Social Studies	Social Studies	Social Studies
Science	Science	Science	Science	Science	Science	Science	Science
Nonfiction Writing Powers	Nonfiction Writing Powers	Nonfiction Writing Powers	Nonfiction Writing Powers	Nonfiction Writing Powers	Nonfiction Writing Powers	Nonfiction Writing Powers	Nonfiction Writing Powers

2 The Components of Nonfiction Writing Power

Children who see themselves as writers from a very early age will develop confidence and competence in the craft of writing. The simple fact is that the more they write, the better they get. Writing for the purpose of producing a published product can be valuable, but an effective writing program also needs to include regular opportunities for students to learn and practice different forms of writing and a variety of writing techniques. In setting up a routine for weekly writing practice, you will help your students move forward in their writing skills and their confidence.

This book is organized around six different nonfiction writing forms: Description, Instruction, Persuasion, Comparison, Explanation, and Nonfiction Narrative. Because the emphasis is on process, rather than product, teachers will need to allow four to six weeks of writing lessons in order for students to become familiar with the intent, structure, and language of each nonfiction form. As mentioned on page 15, it is recommended that teachers choose two or three nonfiction forms to focus on in each grade.

The Nonfiction Writing Power Lesson Framework

Writing Power is organized around a weekly writing schedule based on Donald Grave's writing process:

1. Plan
2. Draft
3. Revise/Edit
4. Conference/Share

For this book, the sequence of lessons do not follow this pattern as strictly; they vary depending on the form you are focusing on and whether or not research is required. The key components of the writing process, however—planning, drafting, and revising—are still incorporated into the guided and independent writing lessons. For each form of nonfiction writing you will be teaching, the lesson framework will follow a pattern that includes

- an introduction to the features of the nonfiction form
- a whole-class write
- independent writing
- writing extensions

At the beginning of the school year, it is important to "train and explain" the routine for each of these stages. The goal is that, by the end of each week, every student will have completed a revised draft.

Introduction to the Nonfiction Power

1–3 lessons (depending on the form and grade level)

As explained on pages 14–15, each nonfiction writing form has distinct features that need to be introduced and taught. It is important for teachers to spend time introducing and explaining these features prior to lauching into the writing lessons.

LESSON OBJECTIVES

- Share anchor books modeling the form.
- Introduce the pattern of the nonfiction structure (see chart on page 18).
- Introduce the key language features of the form.
- Establish the writer's intent or purpose for using the form.
- Develop an anchor chart to list the key features of the nonfiction power (form).

Whole-Class Write

In order to build a strong writing community, we as teachers must be a central part of that community. That means that we must demonstrate to our students that we are writers too. (Dorfman & Cappelli, 2009)

1–2 lessons

Teacher modeling is essential to show students what it looks like when a good writer writes, but it can be challenging for younger students to sit for long periods of time watching someone else write. Combining teacher modeling with student participation provides a more interactive and engaging way for students to witness the development of a piece of writing. Writing in a group setting can help students feel more confident when moving into independent writing. Once students have a basic understanding of the key features (intent, structure, and language) of the nonfiction form, they will participate in a *whole-class write*. This guided lesson is an opportunity for teachers to model the planning and writing of a piece of nonfiction writing in the form the class will be focusing on. These lessons are interactive and provide many opportunities for student participation. Whole-class writes can be done on chart paper or projected onto a screen through a computer, interactive whiteboard, or tablet. Since whole-class writes follow three important stages of the writing process—planning, drafting, revision—they often take two lessons to complete

LESSON OBJECTIVES

- **Interactive Plan:** Combine teacher modeling with class participation to complete a plan for the nonfiction form that follows the structure introduced in the introductory lesson.
- **Interactive Draft:** Combine teacher modeling and class participation to develop a draft piece of writing. Students are encouraged to help generate ideas for the piece.
- **Writing Technique:** Teacher can introduce and/or model a writing technique (see pages 35–44) that can be incorporated into the writing piece.
- **Revision**: Combine teacher modeling and class participation to employ revision and editing techniques.

Independent Write

After partcipating in the whole-class write, students will be ready to begin their own piece of nonfiction writing. It is important to provide several opportunities for students to practice writing using the nonfiction form on a wide variety of topics. These writing activities will vary in length; depending on the topic and form being practiced, students might be required to do some research. Students are encouaged to use the Plan–Draft–Revise model for these writing pieces.

- Students develop a plan based on the nonfiction form they will be working on.
- Writing topics can be teacher- or student-selected.
- Students develop a draft and are encouraged to refer to the anchor chart as a reminder of the features of the form (intent, structure, and language).
- Students are encouraged to incorporate any writing techniques that have been introduced and/or modeled.
- Completed drafts can be shared with a partner or with the class.
- Students spend time revising and editing their writing (see page 24).

Links to Content Areas

Linking content to writing is an important way for students to apply their understanding of nonfiction writing across the curriculum. Once the structure, language, and features of the nonfiction form have been introduced and practiced through several writing pieces, the form can be integrated into a content area you might be focusing on in science and social studies; see lists of examples in the overview that begins each chapter. These writing assignments most likely will require some form of research and therefore might take students several writing periods to complete.

Writing Extensions

Following each independent writing lesson is a list of several writing extensions. These lessons are connected to a topic that lends itself to the nonfiction form and are intendended to be used as further writing practice for students. It is not intended that students complete all of these extensions; a range is provided for teachers to choose from.

Anchor Books

Anyone who knows me professionally or personally, or who has read any of my books, knows how essential children's literature is to me and all aspects of my teaching practice. Picture books are woven through the fabric of almost every lesson I teach. Using picture books as the anchor to my writing lessons helps me to introduce a specific writing technique, text structure, or subject.

There's a Book for That! is the name of the blog of teacher, friend, and fellow book-lover Carrie Gelson. I couldn't agree more with the sentiment! You don't need to look very far through the shelves of any library to know that there is a book for just about everything.

Gone are the days when the nonfiction section of the library was filled with shelves of heavy, dark-bound encyclopedia sets. Nonfiction children's literature has soared in popularity as educational trends try to incorporate more nonfiction literature into content areas. While some students might struggle with accessing information from textbooks that might be written above their reading level, there will likely be a large number of engaging nonfiction books you can use to support their learning. There are excellent nonfiction books out there for just about anything you want to study. Whether your thematic unit is on rainforests, owls, or Canadian pioneers, there is a book available.

As with my other books, I have made every effort to provide lists of picture books to accompany the lessons. I don't mean for teachers to go out and spend thousands of dollars on books. Your local and school library will likely have many of the titles and you can select two or three books for each nonfiction form to start your own collection. Booklists have been organized around the nonfiction writing structures and are listed at the beginning of each chapter. I have also included titles that are connected to some specific lessons. You might find that some of the picture books on my lists are not considered nonfiction, in that the author's intent might be to entertain rather than to inform. However, I have included these books because they can be used as anchor books to support a particular nonfiction writing structure.

As in my earlier books, I have coded the level of the anchor books for each chapter as *P* for *Primary* or *I* for *Intermediate*. However, I don't mean to restrict their use to the levels suggested by the coding. Intermediate books can be used by primary teachers as read-alouds, and primary students should not be discouraged from looking at them. Similarly, books with simpler text labeled *Primary* work well as anchor books for older students, as they model form or structure clearly.

Revision and Editing

No writer publishes his or her first draft. They rework, revise, reorganize, rearrange—there is a lot of *re*-ing that occurs before the writing is finally done. This evolution of a piece of writing is an essential part of the writing process that students need to experience.

Over the years, I have not done a very good job in helping my students learn how to effectively edit. For years, I had the COPS poster up in my classroom and used this as my reference for how to edit. For those of you who are not familiar with this acronym: COPS stands for Capitals, Organization, Punctuation, Spelling, and this process was used by many teachers as a framework for editing. But when I gave it closer examination, I saw that this handy poster was focusing primarily on the mechanics and conventions of writing, which we now understand to be only a portion of what effective writing is. Using the COPS method of revision, a student could plunk a period at the end of one of their sentences and shout, "Done!" Beyond the mechanics of writing, students need to learn how to change, delete, add, rearrange, and reorganize words, sentences, and paragraphs.

I used to use the words "revise" and "edit" interchangeably because I wasn't really clear on the difference. Personal experience has helped me to clarify. As a writer, I have an editor. She is amazing and has helped me through many phases of the editing process: she carefully checks spelling, grammar, punctuation; she makes sure all my charts and student samples are in the correct place and that the page numbers match the references. She also helps me reorganize entire sections. She helps me ensure that my writing is not confusing for my reader; she *edits*. On the other hand, as much as I wish she would sometimes, she does not rewrite for me. She points out places where I need to add, change, or replace text, but she does not do that for me. She does not *revise* for me—I need to do that myself. If you think about the word *revision*, you will see that it is just that, a re-*vision*, in which you make an adjustment to your vision of your piece of writing. It is where the voice of the writer, the style, the intent of a piece of writing are incorporated into the writing. Revision is, as I see it now, a completely separate aspect of writing from editing. It can be done only by the writer, because it was the writer's "vision" in the first place. Revision, therefore, is making my writing interesting and clear for my reader.

My revised version of COPS now includes both the editing and the revising that students need to learn. I have incorporated both into my writing goals, as giving purpose and intent to this stage of the writing process: the purpose of

Claude LaFrance, Grade 4 teacher at Assumption School in Powell River and fellow word collector, introduced me to this important vision of revision.

revision is helping my reader stay interested; the purpose of editing is helping my reader not to be confused.

I have developed primary and intermediate versions of an editing checklist (see below). To help students succeed in this stage of the writing process, I usually introduce one step of the checklist at a time. Students practice the first step for a few weeks before I reveal and introduce the second and third (and fourth) steps, usually through a mini-lesson that involves some teacher modeling. Usually by mid-October, they understand what is expected of them during the editing time of the weekly writing plan (remember that my expectation is that students complete a revised draft by the end of the week). I don't believe that young writers are capable of correcting every mistake they make in a piece of writing, nor should they be expected to. My goal is that they have experienced the process and understand specific things they can do to improve their writing.

This editing checklist is for primary students.

1, 2, 3, 4—EDIT!

1. **Fix** spelling and punctuation.

2. **Change** a word that doesn't sound right.

3. **Erase** a word (or words) that doesn't belong.

4. **Add** a word (or words) to make your writing better.

This editing checklist is for intermediate students.

3, 2, 1—REVISE and EDIT!

3   Fix **3** spelling, punctuation, or spacing mistakes.

2   Add, erase, or replace **2** words.

1   Add to, change, or rearrange **1** sentence.

One-on-One Writing Conferences

I find that one of the most effective ways of getting to know my students as writers is through individual writing conferences. In the business of our days in the classroom, individual conferences can be a wonderful way of connecting to students. I try to meet with each student at least once a month for five to ten minutes. These conferences are often held when the rest of the class is working independently (silent reading is usually a good time!). I try to remember to write the names of two children with whom I will be meeting that day on the board in the morning; if I forget, my students certainly remind me!

During the conference, students will select one of their recent pieces of writing to read aloud to me. Using the Nonfiction Writing Conference Record (page 27), I usually start by asking them a few general questions about the nonfiction form we have been focusing on. I might ask them a few questions about the features, intent, and structure. Students read aloud their piece of writing and, while I'm listening, I try to record a few notes about what I notice in terms of their strengths and weaknesses. Afterward, I may ask them to tell me what they thought was the best part of their piece and which part might need work. I share my thoughts with them and often we set a goal together, based on the things we have noticed in the writing.

Assessment Rubrics

Ongoing assessment of writing is an important step in helping our students move forward in their writing, but it can be a little overwhelming when the marking piles up! I use writing rubrics as a way of tracking the strengths and weaknesses in my students' writing, as well as to provide feedback to students and helping them set goals during one-on-one writing conferences. Because nonfiction forms vary, a one-size-fits-all rubric would not be effective. For each nonfiction form, I have developed an assessment rubric that highlights the important features of the form. I find these rubrics are helpful in determining each student's understanding of the form, as well as the student's development through several writing pieces. The rubrics also help me to notice trends in my class to guide my instruction. If, for example, I notice more than half of my class is struggling with adding interesting details, I might decide to go back and review that lesson with the entire class.

Nonfiction Writing Conference Record

TERM   1   2   3   Student: _____   Date: _____

Text Form: _____   Topic: _____

Teacher	
What is the topic of this piece?	Record student response:
Can you tell me what form of nonfiction writing this is?	Record student response:
What was your intent for his piece? What do you want your reader to know or learn from reading this?	Record student response:
Go ahead and read your piece out loud.	Teacher Notes:
Can you tell me what part of this piece you are most proud of and why?	Record student response:
Can you tell me one part of this piece that you think might need some work and why?	Record student response:
I'm noticing that you have really done a good job of…	Possible suggestions: Check 1 or 2 ☐ Demonstrating understanding of the text structure ☐ Organization – ideas are grouped together ☐ Engaging beginning/ending ☐ Writing makes sense/easy to follow ☐ Using text features to support information ☐ Correct use of capitals and periods ☐ Accurate spelling ☐ Interesting details (not robot writing) ☐ Voice ☐ Using triple-scoop words ☐ Other: _____
Here's something I think might help your writing to get even better:	Possible suggestions: Check 1 or 2 ☐ Demonstrate understanding of the structure ☐ Organization: ideas are grouped together ☐ Great beginning/ending ☐ Writing makes sense/easy to follow ☐ Use of text features ☐ Capitals and periods ☐ Spelling ☐ Variety of sentence length ☐ Interesting details (not robot writing) ☐ Voice ☐ Use of triple-scoop words ☐ Other: _____
Let's set a new goal for your writing. What do you think would help your writing get even better?	Record student's goal here:

© 2014 *Nonfiction Writing Power* by Adrienne Gear. Pembroke Publishers. ISBN 978-1-55138-293-7

3 The Big Picture

Teaching writing with intent and purpose has been an evolution for me. When I began my teaching career more than 25 years ago, I would spend hours at the teacher's store at the end of August, searching for those writing resource books that had it all—the writing topic, the sentence starter, and the lined page I could photocopy: *A Year of Essential Writing Lessons*, *No More Planning—100 Writing Lessons at Your Fingertips!*, *50 Writing Prompts with Graphic Organizers*. Yes, I bought them all. And sadly, I used them to fill my weekly writing blocks with what I thought were productive writing experiences for my students. I was enthusiastic; I was dedicated; I was prepared—but I was not teaching with any sense of purpose or intent.

Fortunately, I have changed the way I look at my instruction—in writing or any subject. Every lesson I teach needs to somehow fit into a bigger picture. And before I even begin to teach a lesson, I need to be able to answer these two questions: *Why am I teaching this?* and *How does it fit?* I am asking this question not only of myself, but also of my students. It is important that they, too, understand why they are learning something and how it fits into the greater whole. My teaching is more about bigger concepts than isolated lessons. And from my vantage point, I believe nonfiction writing instruction is about four big picture concepts: text structure, writer's intent, writer's goals, and writing techniques. Every writing lesson I teach connects to these concepts; therefore, I need my students to have developed an awareness and understanding of each beforehand. These concepts establish purpose for all my writing lessons and go beyond the mini-lessons on voice or indenting paragraphs toward a more important goal: what being a writer is all about. Being a writer is not just about making sure you have capital letters in all the right places or have used a simile in one of your sentences. Being a writer is about understanding that your reader is what matters most; it is about establishing purpose and intent for your reader; it is about keeping your writing interesting so your reader doesn't get bored; it is about making sure your writing makes sense so that your reader doesn't get confused; it is about having a deep understanding of text structure so that your writing is clear for your reader. In the big picture, the reader is the most important part of being a writer.

Nonfiction Text Structure

Five years ago, I did not understand the importance of text structure in writing instruction. I was not aware that teaching students nonfiction text structures was, in fact, the key to their successful writing.

When I think of the division of texts into fiction and nonfiction, I think of a library and its physical division of these types of books to opposite ends of the room. (I have vivid memories of the two sides of the library in my elementary

"I believe that when teachers—myself included—have introduced children to nonfiction writing we have used the word nonfiction far too restrictively."—Tony Stead

See *Writing Power* for more on climbing and walking story structures.

Once writers get an initial understanding of a certain crafted text structure, they will recognize the structure in many other texts. (Ray, 1999: 141)

school: the bright and cheerful fiction side and the "dark side" of the nonfiction shelves.) Dividing the text world into these two equal and opposite sides has helped to introduce a basic understanding of text structure: fiction (the story) vs nonfiction (information). If we delve a little further, we could say that fiction is made up, imaginative, not true; it often evokes more emotions and is primarily read for pleasure. Nonfiction is real, true, not made up; often we read it to learn, to gain knowledge or facts about a particular subject. The clear division makes things simple, neat, and tidy. However, what this "opposite and equal" division of texts in the world has done for many children is mislead them into thinking that there are only two text structures. This is far from correct.

Fiction texts, as I explained in detail in my book *Writing Power*, have two main structures:

- climbing stories, with character/setting/problem/solution and beginning/middle/end: the plot line climbs to a climax and then descends as the story ends
- walking stories, with no problem or solution, giving details, examples, and explanations on a topic: the story walks along a level plane

Nonfiction texts, on the other hand, are a compilation of many different text structures. When referring to the different nonfiction text structures, Lucy Calkins states, "There is no magical list" (1994: 364). Tony Stead, in his book *Is That a Fact?*, writes: "Attempting to list the different purposes for nonfiction is no easy task" (2002: 8). Stead outlines a number of key nonfiction writing forms, or text structures, that he believes children should be exposed to at an early age. These structures include writing to describe, writing to instruct, writing to persuade, and writing to explain.

What has become apparent to me, over years of being in classrooms and working with teachers, is that it is a misconception that story writing is easy. Story writing is, in fact, the most complex of all writing to master because of the components that must be included: characters, setting, plot; beginning, middle, end; problem, solution. To write a story well, the writer has to, in a sense, already know what problem the character is going to experience and how that problem is going to be resolved, long before beginning to write. It is understandable that children struggle with this key element of story writing because it is extremely challenging. Yet for some reason, we tend to focus more on writing stories in primary grades and writing information in intermediate grades.

Nonfiction writing is a collection of more straightforward text structures. Each one has its own unique "skeleton" or shape, and a specific purpose. It is important to establish this with your students early in the school year, before focusing on one specific text structure. This way, they will better see how each form fits into the big picture of nonfiction writing.

Lesson: Introducing Text Structures

This lesson is to provide students with the background information about nonfiction text structures that will be the foundation of subsequent lessons in this book.

- Copy the Text-Structure Title Sort template on page 45; cut out strips and place them in an envelope. Prepare one envelope per group of three or four students.
- Gather different examples of fiction and nonfiction texts from your home or library. If possible, include non-book and digital examples; for example, print

out or project on your interactive whiteboard a blog page, webpage, or Facebook page.

- Separate texts into piles. Make signs that say *Fiction* and *Nonfiction*. In the Fiction pile, include a picture book, a chapter book, and a novel. In the Nonfiction section, include two or three examples of each text structure:
  - Description: e.g., books about animals, insects, countries, space, the human body; blog page describing a book.
  - Instruction: e.g., recipe/cookbooks; how-to books (drawing, crafts); game instructions; magic tricks; online recipes.
  - Persuasion: e.g., travel brochures; catalogues; an online review of a book or movie; any book with a persuasive title: *I Wanna Iguana, I Wanna New Room, Can I Have A Pet?*
  - Comparison: any text that compares two or more things.
  - Explanation: nonfiction texts that have "why" in the title: e.g., *Why Do Snakes Shed Their Skin?*; *Why Does Popcorn Pop?*; *Why is The Polar Bear's World Melting?*
  - Nonfiction Narrative: e.g., biographies; newspaper reports; social media pages; books on events in the past, such as the sinking of the Titanic.

- Begin the lesson:

  Today we are going to explore different kinds of texts. I went to the library and gathered a lot of examples of different kinds of texts that I will be sharing with you. But before I show them to you, we are going to do a little sorting exercise.

- Divide the class into groups and give one envelope to each group. Explain that inside the envelope are different titles of books. Their job is to sort the book titles. They can make as many different groups as they like, but must be able to explain what each group has in common. Allow time for students to sort book titles.
- Ask groups to explain how they sorted (answers will vary, but usually the students sort into Fiction and Nonfiction).
- Tell students you have brought in some different books to share. Begin with the fiction pile; show the books to the students and ask them the following questions:

  What do we know about these kinds of books? (they are fiction, stories)
  Would you agree that they are all different? (yes, different stories, different characters, etc.)
  Even though they are all different stories, what do they have in common? (text structure)

- Explain that every fiction story shares one of two common structures. I like to use the analogy of a human body: on the outside we all look different, but on the inside we all have the same skeleton.
- Move on to the nonfiction pile:

  Now we are going to look at some nonfiction books. Fiction texts have two basic text structures, but nonfiction books have several.
  (Show Description books to the students.)
  Here are some nonfiction books. This one is about ladybugs; this one is about

Remind students of the text structures of a story: a "climbing" structure has character and setting, problem and solution, and a beginning, middle, and end; a "walking" structure has a topic, followed by details and examples. Remind students that writers writing stories need to use one of these structures as the skeleton of their stories, but they add their own ideas on the outside to make their stories different.

bears; this one is about Africa; and this one is about the planet Jupiter. All these books are nonfiction. They are all about different topics, but they all share the same skeleton or text structure. These types of nonfiction books are called *description* books because they describe or tell about something—all different topics but all the same structure. A writer who wants to tell about a topic needs to use this text structure.

- Continue to introduce the other forms of nonfiction in the same manner, emphasizing that each book is nonfiction, each is about a different topic, but they all share a similar text structure.
- Create a chart on the board as you introduce each structure.

SAMPLE TEXT STRUCTURE CHART

Fiction Text Structure	Nonfiction Text Structure
Climbing Story • Character, setting, problem, solution • Beginning–middle–end **Walking Story** • Topic, detail, detail, detail	**Description** – tells reader details about one topic **Instruction** – tells reader how to do something **Persuasion** – presents an opinion or point of view to the reader, or attempts to convince the reader of something **Comparison** – tells the reader how two things are the same and how they are different **Explanation** – explains how or why something happens **Nonfiction Narratives** – true stories that tell the reader the events and significance of a person's life, or other events

For younger students who might not be able to do the Title Sort independently, teachers can make a set of cards with different titles and do the activity as a class.

This sample is by a student in Grade 2.

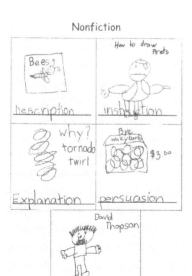

- Invite students to go back to their book title sort and reorganize the titles to reflect their new understanding of text structures. Students can fill in the Nonfiction Text Structures graphic organizer on page 46 or glue their strips onto an enlarged version of the chart. Primary students can draw visuals to represent each text structure (see sample at left).
- Review with students what they learned about text structure:
  - A text structure is how a piece of writing is organized.
  - Fiction texts have two main structures: climbing or walking.
  - There are several different nonfiction structures: description, instruction, comparison, persuasion, explanation, nonfiction narrative.
  - Writers need to know the structure before they begin to write.
  - This year, we will be learning about different nonfiction text structures and practicing writing in these different forms.

LESSON EXTENSION

If you have or are able to borrow a class set of *Chirp* or *Chickadee* magazine from your school library, you can use them as resources for students to practice identifying different text structures within one magazine. These magazines often include a story, cartoon, poem, recipe, instructions on how to make or do something, a description and photographs of an animal or insect, and a scientific explanation for something. I like to pair up students and give them sticky notes to label and tag pages as they go through the magazine. Even if the magazines appear too simple for older students, it is still good practice for them to try to identify the different text structures within the magazine.

Writer's Intent

Whether writing a novel, a news article, a recipe book, a blog post, an encyclopedia entry, a letter of complaint, or a tweet, a writer will consciously or unconsciously ask him/herself, *Why am I writing this?* Depending on what the writer is writing and who the reader is, intention changes. In consciously establishing intent prior to writing—a step I believe should be included in every writing lesson—we teach the importance of establishing the link between the writer and the reader.

Lesson: Introducing Writer's Intent

- Begin the lesson:

  I've been thinking a lot about writing lately and about all the different kinds of writing there are in the world: stories, biographies, newspaper reports, recipes, blogs, information books, e-mails, tweets, poems, songs. Let's brainstorm a list of *What Do Writer's Write?*

- Have students brainstorm in partners and then invite them to share their ideas. Record their answers on a chart or interactive whiteboard. Challenge your students to fill up an entire chart stand with answers.

  Now we've just talked about the *what* part of writing. Now I'd like us to think about the *why* of writing. Why do writer's write? What is the reason a writer would write a recipe or a story or news report?

- Record answers on a chart paper or interactive whiteboard.

  WHY do writer's write?
  - To entertain (make you laugh or make you feel scared)
  - To inform (share facts and information)
  - To "wow" (surprise or shock you with astonishing facts)
  - To describe (give details about something)
  - To persuade (share an opinion, convince you to do something)
  - To explain something (tell how or why something happens)
  - To instruct (tell how to make something, do something, or achieve something)
  - To transform (nudge the reader's thinking)

  Explain that the *why* of writing is called *writer's intent*, that "intent" is another word for purpose or goal.

- Give some examples of intentions in everyday activities:

  What would my intent be…
  - if I run hard in soccer? (to score a goal, win the game)
  - if I start exercising every day? (to get fit, lose weight, be healthy)
  - if I share toys with my brother? (to be kind, stop him from crying)

- Explain that if a writer thinks about his or her intent before writing, it can really help the writer stay focused on the reader. Writers who ask themselves *What do I want my reader to learn, know, understand, do, or think when they read this?* before they write are showing intent. Explain that this year they will be thinking about writer's intent before they write.

Writer's Goals

The biggest shift in my teaching practice in writing instruction since publishing *Writing Power* has been helping students change from focusing on "my writing" to focusing on "my reader." This seemingly simple shift has made an enormous difference in the way I teach writing. For years, my writing instruction had been focusing on making students' writing better. But the purpose behind making writing better was "I am telling you to make it better" or "You want to get a better mark." Switching the focus to the reader—the person on the receiving end of the writer's words—has brought purpose and intent to my lessons. It has also helped give my students a different motivation for improving their writing. They no longer write for a mark or to hand in an assignment—they write to engage and connect to their readers.

Since *Writing Power* was published, I have spent many hours in classrooms talking to students about "becoming writers." I have focused a great deal on the *why* of writing and the importance of connecting and engaging with our readers through our writing. I use the catch phrase *We write to invite thinking* frequently during my writing lessons. Many of my mini-lessons focus on writing techniques, such as adding interesting details, using similes, adding voice to writing. Over time, I have heard myself repeating, "This writing technique can really help to invite your readers in and help them connect to your writing."

I am always trying to find ways to simplify concepts to help my students understand something more clearly. I developed the My Writing Goals chart (see below) as a way of simplifying writing for students and to help me reinforce a big-picture concept that can be as relevant to a Grade 1 class as in a Grade 11 creative writing class.

My Writing Goals	
To make sure my **reader** is interested • interesting words • interesting details • similes • voice • personification • using the senses • using text features (when appropriate)	To make sure my **reader** is not confused • spelling • punctuation • spacing • organization • clarity, making sense • neat printing • page numbers

Lesson: Introducing Writer's Goals

• Begin the lesson:

People write for different reasons. Some people like to write for themselves—they write in a diary or a journal to keep track of their thoughts and feelings, but it's not really for anyone else to read. This is what we call *private writing*. The other kind of writing people do is writing for someone else to read. We call this *public writing*. It means the writer has something to say that he or she wants someone else to read. Most of the writing we learn to do in school is public writing because other people are going to read it.

Remind students that good writers invite their readers into their writing. A writer's goal is for someone to read and enjoy what he or she has written.

• Ask students if they have ever started reading something but didn't finish. Ask them what might be a reason for someone to stop reading something? (not interested; not interesting, confusing).

If writing is not interesting, I usually don't want to keep reading it. So, as a writer, I know it is important for me to make my writing interesting. If it's not, then my reader might not want to keep reading.

• Write *My Writing Goals* at the top of a T-chart on the board, a chart, or the interactive whiteboard.

I have only two goals as a writer but both are very important. The first is to make sure my writing is interesting for my reader.
(Write *Interesting* at the top of the left column)
If my writing is not interesting, what is my reader likely to do? (stop reading) As a writer, I certainly don't want my reader to get bored and stop reading! So I need to think, *What are some things I can do to keep my writing interesting?*
(Begin to brainstorm and list in left column *interesting words, interesting details, similes, voice, the senses*)
These are called writer's techniques and knowing how to use them when you write can really help make your writing more interesting for your reader.

- Continue the lesson:

  > Now as a writer, I have a second very important goal. I'm going to show you something that sometimes happens to me when I'm reading. Watch my face as I read.
  > (Pretend to read something and then model a confused expression. Keep reading and keep being confused.)
  > Now what are you noticing? What are you inferring?

- Explain that this is called your "confused face" and it happens sometimes when you read.

  > Have you ever read something and felt confused? What happens if you are really confused when you are reading? (often we will stop reading) So, as a writer, I have a second goal. To make sure my reader is not confused! How do you think a writer might reach that goal?

  Write *Not Confusing* at the top of the right column. Discuss things that could make writing confusing. List *spelling, spacing, punctuation, organization, makes sense, staying on topic.*

- End the lesson:

  > Whenever we write, it is important that we always try to think about these two goals so that our reader will be interested in what we have to say and not be confused. This year, we are going to be working on ways to reach at least one of these goals every time we write.

LESSON EXTENSION

Students can create their own Writer's Goals chart.

Tools for Meeting Our Writing Goals

Writing techniques are the specific writing skills or tools that writers use to enhance their craft. All writers need to learn and practice techniques to help engage their readers and improve the quality of their writing. It is sometimes difficult for children to focus on several techniques at one time, so students are taught the techniques over the course of the year and are given opportunities to practice and apply them in their weekly pieces of writing.

As a new technique is introduced, it can be listed on a Nonfiction Writing Power anchor chart. Nonfiction writing techniques include

- using nonfiction text features
- adding details
- using "triple-scoop" words
- making comparisons
- voice in writing
- hooking your reader with a good introduction
- organization

In *Writing Power*, I focused on a range of these Technical Powers to be taught as mini-lessons and incorporated into the weekly pieces of writing. Nonfiction writing also includes some specific technques that help to enhance the style. In my experience, good writing is good writing, regardless of whether you are describing an imaginary character or a poison dart frog.

In her recent book *Genre Connections,* Tanny McGregor suggests handing out seed packages to pairs of students as a way of introducing text features. How much information can you gather from the features on the seed package? Brilliant!

Lesson: Nonfiction Text Features

The most significant difference between the way fiction texts are written and the way nonfiction texts are written can be seen as soon as you open the covers of each and compare the pages visually. The pages of a fiction book give the reader either text with illustrations or, in the case of a novel, text only. A nonfiction book, however, generally has a visual layout that represents information in a variety of different ways, through both text and text features. Nonfiction features are an essential part of informational texts, as they help readers better locate, navigate, access, and ultimately understand the information. It is this presentation of information that writers of information need to incorporate into their work. In my book *Nonfiction Reading Power*, Zooming In to nonfiction features is one of the reading strategies I discuss. Readers of nonfiction need to focus their attention on these features in order to locate and access information while they are reading. As writers of nonfiction, students need to know how to create these features as an effective way of representing information to their readers.

- Pair up several fiction and nonfiction books from the library, or use pre-paired sets of readers, such as the Take Two books (Wright Group). Have enough for one pair of books for each pair of students in your class.
- Hold up two books on the same topic: one fiction and one nonfiction. (I like to use *Make Way for Ducklings* by Robert McClosky and *Watch and Grow Ducklings* from DK Publishing.) Ask students what they notice. (Both books are about ducks; one has a photo, the other has illustrations; one is a story, the other is real.) Depending on the grade level you teach, you can introduce or review the terms *fiction* and *nonfiction*.
- On a large Venn diagram, write *Fiction* and *Nonfiction* on the outer sections; write *Both* on the inner section.
- Do a quick walk-and-talk of both books, pointing out similarities and differences as you go. For example, "In this book, I'm noticing a lot of text and illustrations." "In this book I notice the text is in different places on the page."
- Have students discuss similarities and differences between the two books with a partner. Invite students to share out and add ideas onto the Venn diagram.
- Continue the lesson:

  Now we know that fiction and nonfiction texts are not only about different things, but they also look very different. We've noticed that pages of nonfiction texts have a lot of things going on: maps, charts, fact boxes, headings, captions. These are called *nonfiction features* and they are a very important part of nonfiction writing.

- Create an anchor chart listing the nonfiction features that students noticed in left column. Brainstorm what the features might be used for in the right column.

NONFICTION FEATURES ANCHOR CHART

Nonfiction Feature	Purpose
Map	To show location: e.g., habitat of animal
Web	List of any kind: for example, a list of food an animal eats or its enemies

Nonfiction Feature	Purpose
Diagram, Labels	Description
Fact Box	Interesting facts
Flow Chart	To show how things work together: e.g., life cycle
Chart	To sort details: e.g., facts about different species
Labels, Captions	To explain a diagram or picture
Timeline	Sequential events or dates
Diagram with Labels	Comparisons

- Continue the lesson:

  Why are nonfiction features are important? Why do nonfiction texts have these features but fiction texts don't?

- Make a web. Write *What are Text Features For?* in the centre. Add ideas to web, including *organize information, locate information, navigate information, highlight information, access information*, explaining as you go.
- Ask students why a nonfiction writer might use a text feature instead of writing. Explain you will be doing an exercise to find out why.
- Read aloud "Cats and Bunnies" on page 47 and ask someone to time how long it takes for you to read it.
- Record the time it took to read the passage.
- Show the Venn diagram from page 47. Ask students to "read" the Venn diagram, and time their reading.
- Compare the two times: which took longer? Explain that, with the Venn diagram, you were able to "access" the information much more quickly, with the information going from the text into your brain in the most efficient way.
- Explain that the reason nonfiction writers use text features is that they make information easier for their readers to access.
- Explain that students will be learning to use text features in their writing to help readers access facts more quickly and easily.

Lesson: Interesting Details

- Write the following sentences on the board or interactive whiteboard:

  A bear is a mammal.
  A bear has fur.
  A bear has sharp teeth and claws.
  A bear lives in the forest.
  A bear eats fish and berries.
  Many bears live in North America.

- Begin the lesson:

  Today, I wanted to share some information about bears with you.
  (Read the sentences out loud)

- Ask students what they noticed. (Text repeated "a bear" a lot; sounds like a list; not very interesting.)
- Remind students about one of your writing goals: *Make sure my writing is interesting for my reader.* Explain that when a nonfiction writer includes only the facts about a topic but not any interesting details, the reader will likely start feeling a little bored. It's important for a writer to follow these steps: *Write a fact. Add a detail.* Have students repeat this phrase a few times.
- Ask students if they think your bear writing is interesting and how you might make it more interesting. (By adding details)
- Model adding a detail to one of the sentences:

Teacher Model

  A bear is a mammal. That means it is covered in fur, and that the mother gives birth to live babies and feeds the babies milk.

- Ask students to choose another sentence and see if they can add a detail to the fact. Have them practice in their heads first, then share with a partner. Invite some to share out with the class.
- End the lesson:

  One of the ways writers can make their writing interesting to their readers is by adding interesting details. This is especially true when you are sharing facts about a topic.

- Add *Adding Details* to the My Writing Goals anchor chart (see page 34).

LESSON EXTENSION

I've noticed that, when children are learning to add details to facts, they tend to overuse *because* and *and*. Often these transition words do not lead to interesting or informative details.

  Bears attack people because they are mean.

There are certain words, however, that lead to more interesting details: *if, when, sometimes, often, usually, for example.* I like to introduce students to these words and have them practice using them instead of *because* or *and*.

  *Bears attack people. **Often** a bear attacks if they think their babies are being threatened.*

Lesson: Triple-Scoop Words

One of the most effective technique lessons from *Writing Power* was the one involving triple-scoop words. Students and teachers alike seemed to like using this catch phrase to remind young writers to focus on word choice.

Whether you are writing fiction or nonfiction, choosing interesting and sophisticated words in your writing enhances the quality. I talk about *triple-scoop words,* comparing words to ice cream, referring to how I would always order the "kiddie cone" for my sons: a little lump of ice cream in a styrofoam cone. My boys would never be satisfied after eating the ice cream and wished they had been able to get a triple-scoop cone: three scoops of different flavors in a waffle cone. Sometimes, when reading student writing, I notice a lot of "little lump" words of description. These words don't really leave me feeling satisfied. Our goal is to use triple-scoop words in our writing so that our writing is interesting and our reader feels satisfied.

- Write the following sentences on the board or interactive whiteboard:

   Most spiders make nice silk to make big webs for getting prey.
   Most spiders make delicate strands of silk to create sturdy webs for capturing prey.

- Ask students which sentence is more interesting to read and why. (the second, because it has interesting words: *delicate, sturdy, capturing*)
- Remind students that one of goals we are working on is making sure our writing is interesting to read. Using interesting, triple-scoop words instead of single-scoop words can help make the reader stay interested and feel satisfied!
- Copy and distribute the Nonfiction Triple-Scoop Word Chart from page 48. Invite students to pair up and to complete the page in partners. The single-scoop words can be adapted to the nonfiction form of writing that you are working on.
- Add *Triple-Scoop Words* to the My Writing Goals anchor chart (see page 34).

LESSON EXTENSION

Put up a Triple-Scoop Words list in your classroom. You and your students can continue to add triple-scoop words as you come across them in other books you read.

Sue Stevenson, a principal in Vancouver, had a triple-scoop word challenge at her school. Every class received a "cone" with a single-scoop word on it.

Classes tried to fill their cones with as many triple-scoop words as they could!

Lesson: Comparison Using Similes

Anchor Books

Barbara Brenner, *Thinking About Ants* (P)
Ben Hillman, *How Fast Is It?*; *How Big Is It?*; *How Strong Is It?* (I)

Steve Jenkins, *Hottest, Coldest, Highest, Deepest*; *Big and Little*; *Biggest, Strongest, Fastest*; *Actual Size*; *Just a Second* (P, I)

P = primary
I = intermediate
Note that book level is a suggestion only; all books can be used at any level. See page 23.

Similes are a figure of speech often associated with desciptions in narrative or fictional text: e.g., *Her eyes glowed like emeralds.* Similes help a reader visualize and connect with the text. While they tend to be used primarily in fictional writing, this technique can be introduced to student writers of nonfiction through a nonfiction version of a simile; namely, a comparison. When using a simile, the writer is required to use the words "as" or "like"; this is not necessary when writing a comparison. But the idea of comparing two things that are similar to enhance the reader's understanding certainly holds true for both. Writers of nonfiction often use comparisons in their descriptions to provide readers with a clearer image, inviting the reader to visualize the information by connecting the unknown fact with something he/she might already know.

- Write the following sentences on the board or interactive whiteboard:

   Each flower has five petals, about the size of dinner plates.
   Did you know the largest ant in the world is only about the size of a person's thumb?

It's hard to fathom the vastness of the universe or the size of a molecule. But when you compare such things to other, familiar objects, readers can use what they know to understand the unfamiliar. (Fletcher & Portalupi, 2001: 43)

Nonfiction children's author Steve Jenkins is the master of comparisons. Not only does he include comparisons in his texts, but he also creates visual comparisons in his illustrations.

Some people might think that penguins waddle slowly but, in fact, they walk about as fast as a person walks.
If a tarantula did bite you, its bite would feel like a bee sting.

- Begin the lesson:

  One of our goals, as nonfiction writers, is to always try to make our writing interesting for our reader. I have some interesting sentences that I have borrowed from some information books. While I read them to you, I'd like you to be thinking about what they all have in common.

- Read the sentences aloud to the class. Ask students what they notice about the sentences. (They all include a comparison or simile.)
- Explain that a comparison is when a writer compares two things that are similar when they are describing something.

  In nonfiction writing, comparisons are often used in descriptions about size, speed, distance, appearance, and texture.

  For those students who are familiar with the term *simile*, explain that a comparison is very much like a simile, except that it does not have to include "like" or "as."
- Ask students why nonfiction writers might use comparisons in their writing. (to help their readers understand the information better; to help readers visualize)
- Pass out the Dare to Compare chart from page 49 and invite students (in pairs or individuals) to complete the page.
- Add *Comparisons* to the My Writing Goals anchor chart (see page 34) and encourage students to use comparisons in their descriptions.

Lesson: Voice

Anchor Books

Judy Allan, *Are You A Bee?* (Backyard Books: series includes spider, ant, grasshopper, ladybug) (P, I)
Nicola Davies, *One Tiny Turtle* (or any book by this author) (P, I)

Martin Jenkins, *The Emperor's Egg* (P, I)
Martin Jenkins, *Chameleons are Cool!* (P, I)
Karen Wallace, *Gentle Giant Octopus* (or any book by this author) (P, I)

P = primary
I = intermediate

Voice in writing is what draws readers in, engages them, and invites them into the writer's world. It has been defined as the fingerprint that a writer leaves on the page. With nonfiction writing, according to Ralph Fletcher and JoAnn Portalupi (2001), there is a tendency for younger students to list facts, excluding the voice and emotion that draw readers in. Once students have gathered facts about a topic, they can reread them, adding personal thoughts and feelings. Fact and thoughts can be combined to help students create their own voice when sharing their information orally with a partner before writing.

It is the voices of nonfiction writers that draw us into their world. Their interests and the things they know best can also become things we know and love if we hear their voices inside our head and our heart. (Dorfmann & Capelli, 2009: 188)

Some nonfiction authors are masters of drawing in the reader. I often turn to books by Martin Jenkins, Nicola Davies, and Karen Wallace as my anchor books for this lesson. Take every opportunity to read aloud from these books to provide your students with excellent examples of voice in nonfiction writing.

- Begin the lesson:

  Today we are going to learn a writing technique that we can use to help make our information more interesting for our reader.

- Remind students that one of our writing goals is to always try to keep our readers interested in our writing. Explain that sometimes when we are writing a lot of facts and information, it can sound boring.

  Nonfiction writing is factual but it doesn't have to be boring! Using your writing voice to "talk" to your reader is the best way to keep your reader interested in what you have to say.

- Tell students you are going to read aloud two examples of information writing. Both passages are about the same topic (Emperor Penguins) but they are written in different styles. Tell students they should be thinking about which passage is more interesting and why.

Passage 1

After the female Emperor Penguin lays her egg, she heads off to the sea. Female Emperor Penguins spend most of their winter finding food to store as fat. Male Emperor Penguins take the role of taking care of the egg. They protect the egg from the wind and cold by sitting on it for approximately two months.

Passage 2

Soon after a female Emperor penguin lays her egg, she turns and waddles off to sea. That's where female Emperor penguins spend most of the winter—swimming about, getting as fat as they can, eating as much as they can and generally having a very nice time! This leaves the father penguin stuck on the ice with his egg. And what better way to stop the egg from getting cold but to rest it on your feet and tuck it right up under your tummy? Which is just what the father penguin does—and that's where he stays—FOR TWO WHOLE MONTHS! Can you imagine standing around in the freezing cold with an egg under your feet for two MONTHS??? (Martin Jenkins, *The Emperor's Egg*)

- Read aloud the passages. Ask students which passage was more interesting. (Passage 2) Why? (because it sounded like the author was talking to you, rather than telling you)
- Explain that the second passage effectively uses voice—the voice of the writer talking to the reader, adding reactions and thoughts about the facts, not just stating the facts. Explain that using voice in writing makes reading much more interesting to read and keeps the reader engaged.
- Use Finding Your Voice on page 50 as a practice exercise for students finding their voice.
- Using a read-aloud/think-aloud technique, read the passage out loud with the students and model jotting down thoughts and reactions to the facts in the sidebar.
- Invite students to do the same in partners.

- Model how to rewrite the text, using the facts but adding your thoughts:

> *Chameleons are a kind of lizard. They have bumpy skin and bulgy eyes, like frogs. Chameleons always look a little grumpy because their mouths turn down at the corners. Imagine pouting ALL day, even when you are happy!*

- Invite students to do the same on their papers, combining the facts with their thoughts and feelings when rewriting the passage.
- Add *Voice* to the My Writing Goals anchor chart (see page 34).

Lesson: Introductions to Hook Your Reader

Think of [an introduction] as shaking hands with a new person, your reader, for the first time. It's an important first connection. (Fletcher & Portalupi, 2001: 57)

In *Nonfiction Matters*, Stephanie Harvey encourages us to think of writers as fishermen: "They cast out their first line of words in the hopes of hooking the reader and reeling him into the text." (1998: 150)

- Attach a piece of string to a ruler. Attach a small magnet to the end of the string. (Try to find a U-shaped magnet—they work the best and are the easiest to tie on!)
- Copy Hooking Your Reader on page 51, cut out the strips and attach a paper clip to each. Scatter the strips on the floor.
- Begin the lesson:

> Today we are going to learn a new writing technique that is going to help us reach our first writing goal: making sure our writing is interesting for our reader.

- Ask if anyone has ever gone fishing before:

> What are you trying to do when you go fishing? (catch a fish) How do you do that? (uses bait to hook the fish)

- Explain that writers are a little bit like fishermen: they want to hook their readers right away and reel them in with their writing.
- Ask for a student volunteer to "go fishing." Explain that you have written some beginning sentences on pieces of paper. Invite the student to fish for one, to hook it with the magnet and reel it in.
- Once the student has "caught" a sentence, invite the student to read the sentence out loud to the class (or read it for him/her).
- Ask the class if they are hooked: Do they want to keep reading that piece of writing or would they toss it back? Post the sentence on the board or chart paper under *Hooked* or *Toss Back*.
- Continue until all the sentences are caught.
- Discuss what the writer did to hook the reader. Create an anchor chart:

To "hook" your reader, start with

- a question
- a surprising fact
- a visual image
- a sound or someone speaking
- using your writing voice to talk directly to the reader

- Reflection: You never get a second chance to make a first impression. This applies to writing because if the reader is not hooked from the beginning, they will probably not want to keep reading.

- Add *hooking your reader* to the My Writing Goals anchor chart (see page 34).

Lesson: Organization

Grouping ideas together and keeping them organized in paragraphs is likely the most challenging, yet most important, skill in writing. Students often start writing about one thing, get sidetracked, start writing about something else, and then suddenly switch back to their original topic.

My Grade 2 teacher had an obsession with indenting. She made us all use two finger spaces at the beginning of each paragraph and would walk around doing spot checks to make sure we were using two fingers, not one! I certainly learned one small component of paragraph writing, but I missed the most essential aspect: why we were indenting in the first place. Understanding the text structure you are going to be using for your writing can certainly help to keep your ideas organized. But, aside from learning how to indent, developing a clear concept of what a paragraph is and how to group your ideas using them is an essential skill in becoming a writer.

You can use this lesson, with its analogy of a chest of drawers, to teach the concept of a paragraph even before referring to it as a paragraph.

- Begin the lesson:

  So far, we have learned several writing techniques that have helped us make sure our writing is interesting for our readers. I've been noticing some great comparisons, interesting details, and triple-scoop words in your writing. Today I want to talk about our other goal: Making sure our reader is not confused. Sometimes when I read your writing, my face starts looking like this (demonstrate a confused look while pretending to read a paper). This is my confused face!

- Read the sample paragraph, using your confused face.

> Frogs are amphibians that live near water such as ponds, rivers, or swamps. Frogs have bumpy skin and bulgy eyes. My grandma has bulgy eyes too. Sometimes when she's mad her eyes are very bulgy. She gets mad when I burp at the table. Frogs like to swim. I like to swim too, except when water goes up my nose. Frogs are green and sometimes come in different colors. Frogs have long tongues and they lay eggs. When the egg hatches, a tadpole comes out. Frogs eat flies and other bugs. Tadpoles grow legs and then turn into frogs. Frogs can jump high but my grandma can't. She can't really jump at all, because she uses a walker.

- Ask students what was confusing about the writing. (Ideas are all mixed up and sometimes off-topic.) Remind students that good writers try to organize their ideas so that their readers don't get confused.
- Ask students to think about their dresser drawers at home in their bedroom. Ask what the drawers are for. (to organize your clothes) Ask them to imagine if there were no drawers and all their clothes were kept inside one box, all mixed up together. What would happen if you were trying to find something: (It would be confusing.)

- Invite students to visualize opening their first drawer and looking inside. What do you see? (socks) Just one sock or many?
- Now have them visualize closing the drawer and opening the next one. What's inside? (underwear) Just one pair or many?
- Repeat this a few more times, taking students mentally through their different drawers.
- Draw a large dresser drawer on the board or interactive whiteboard. Explain that writers use drawers when they write. If your students are older, explain that a drawer is actually a paragraph.

The drawer analogy is an effective visual to use when teaching all the nonfiction forms. Depending on the form you are teaching, the number of drawers and how you fill them will vary, but the concept is one that can be applied to all the forms.

Writers think of a topic first—let's say I'm going to write about frogs. I first have to decide what I'm going to put inside each of my drawers. What would my reader like to know about frogs? Maybe my first drawer will be about what they look like. My second drawer might be about where they live. My third drawer might be about their food; my next drawer about their life cycle. And then I might have one last drawer with interesting facts.

Now I know what is in each of my drawers, my next job is to fill each drawer with sentences. So I'm going to open my first drawer and fill it with sentences about what frogs look like. I might write about their size, skin, eyes, legs, and color. Just like your sock drawer, you have more than one sock in there, but they are all socks. My first drawer has more than one sentence in it, but they are all about what the frog looks like. Now I'm finished, so I'm going to close the drawer, leave a space in my writing, and open the next drawer. Now I'm going to fill this drawer with sentences about where frogs live…

Continue on in this fashion until all drawers are filled.

I often refer back to the drawer analogy when I'm conferencing with students: "You have only one sock in that drawer!" or "That sentence is in the wrong drawer!" or "That sentence is in the wrong room!"

- The number of drawers can change to reflect how many paragraphs you are going to include. Depending on the age of your students, you would eventually introduce the ideas of introductory sentences and indenting.
- Add Organization to the My Writing Goals anchor chart (see page 34) in the right column (*Make sure my reader is not confused*).

Text-Structure Title Sort

How to Make Simple Soups	*Diary of a Wimpy Kid*	*Why Do Snakes Shed Their Skin?*	*Big Cats to Fear Vol. 1*
Guinness Book of World Records	*The Three Little Pigs*	*How To Draw Classic Cars*	*Healthy Recipes for Your Family*
Tornados—Explaining the Mysteries of the Sky	*My Brother Is an Alien*	*You Can Do Magic Tricks!*	*SPAIN People and Culture*
The Beetle Book	*Why Do We Burp, Yawn and Sneeze?*	*Disneyland Survival Guide*	*COOKIE COOK BOOK*
How Do Rainbows Form?	*Why Do Leaves Change Color? (And other questions about the seasons)*	*New York—The Best City on Earth*	*Harry Potter and the Philosopher's Stone*
Terry Fox—A Story of Hope	*Wayne Gretzky—Life of a Hockey Legend*	*Life and Times of Barack Obama*	*Goldilocks and the Three Bears*
Why Does Popcorn Pop? (and other kitchen questions)	*How to Take Care of Your Pet*	*On A Beam of Light: The Story of Albert Einstein*	*Magic Treehouse #19 Tigers at Twilight*
HANDS FREE: Why Cell Phones Should Be Banned From Cars	*Dogs Are the World's Best Pet*	*Backyard Bugs (creepy crawlies you find in your yard!)*	*HOW to GROW and EAT GREEN*
I Wanna PUPPY, PLEEEEEEZZZ!	*All About Puppies*	*Bears of Canada*	*Christmas Crafts to Make and Share*
Bunnies and Cats Which pet would you pick?	*Turtles and Tortoises*	*Rugby and Football Same or Different?*	*iPhone or Samsung – which do you prefer?*

Nonfiction Text Structures

Name: _____

Description	Instruction
Persuasion	**Comparison**
Explanation	**Nonfiction Narrative**

Comparing Cats and Bunnies

Cats and Bunnies

Cats and bunnies have many similarities and differences. Both are mammals that are covered in fur. Both also have whiskers and a tail, and are similar in size. People enjoy having both cats and bunnies as pets. They are relatively clean animals and come in a variety of colors.

When comparing differences in appearance, you would notice the different ears and tails. Cats have short triangle ears, while most bunnies have long ears. Cats have long thin tails, while bunnies have short fluffy tails. Cats make sounds like meows, purring, or yowling, while bunnies don't make any sound at all. Cats move smoothly, but bunnies hop. Cats like to eat mice but bunnies eat vegetables, such as carrots and lettuce. Cats have sharp claws and sharp teeth, but bunnies have long, square teeth. Cats are a symbol of Halloween and bunnies are a symbol of Easter.

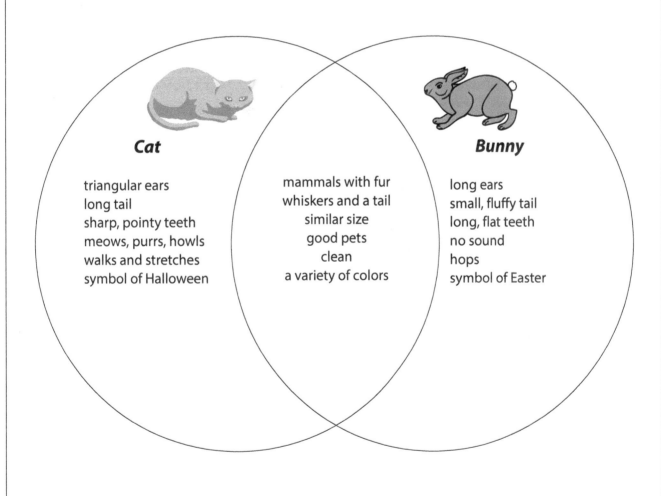

Cat

triangular ears
long tail
sharp, pointy teeth
meows, purrs, howls
walks and stretches
symbol of Halloween

mammals with fur
whiskers and a tail
similar size
good pets
clean
a variety of colors

Bunny

long ears
small, fluffy tail
long, flat teeth
no sound
hops
symbol of Easter

© 2014 *Nonfiction Writing Power* by Adrienne Gear. Pembroke Publishers. ISBN 978-1-55138-293-7

Nonfiction Triple-Scoop Word Chart

Name: _____

Single Scoop	Triple Scoop
hot	*sweltering, melting, scorching, roasting*
cold	
wet	
scary	
big	
small	
look for	
tired	
hungry	
eat	
slow	
fast	
really	
lots	
run	
walk	
catch	
hard	

Dare to Compare

Name: _____

Compare This....	To That...
A cat's tongue is rough	*like sandpaper.*
A dinosaur's tooth is as big as	*a corn on the cob.*
A bee sting feels like…	
A frog's skin is bumpy like…	
A giraffe is as tall as…	
A lady bug is about the size of…	
A blue whale can eat up to…	
An ant is as small as a…	
A _____ is as busy as…	
A _____ is soft like …	
A _____ is as wise as…	
A _____ is quick as…	
The wettest place on earth is Tutunendo, Colombia, with almost 40 meters of rain every year. That is like…	
The bee hummingbird is only 7 cm long, about the size of a…	
An anaconda snake can grow to be 7 meters long. That's as long as…	
An ostrich egg weighs 1.5 kg, about the size of…	
The atlas moth's wingspread is 30 cm across. That's as big as…	
The Goliath frog is almost 1 meter long, which is as long as…	
The Galapagos tortoise lives 150 years. That's about…	
A flea can jump 20 cm in the air. That's…	

Finding Your Voice

Name: _____

Read the paragraph below about chameleons. As you read, record your thoughts and reactions beside the passage. Share the facts and reactions with your partner.

Chameleons are a kind of lizard. They have bumpy skin and bulgy eyes and their mouths turn down at the corners. Some chameleons change color when they're angry, hot, cold, or sick. Other chameleons don't change color at all. Chameleons move slowly along branches, using their pincer-shaped feet for holding on. Unlike humans, chameleons can move each eye separately and in different directions in their sockets. They have long tongues that they use to catch insects.	My thoughts, reactions, connections, feelings:

Combine the FACTS and your VOICE to rewrite the information below:

_____

_____

_____

_____

_____

_____

_____

_____

Hooking Your Reader

Sharks are ocean animals. They swim in warm waters and they have sharp teeth and sometimes can kill people. Sharks are interesting and now I am going to tell you about them.
Hello. My name is Kelly and this is my report about sharks.
Ahhhh! A shark! Swim for your life!
I chose to write my report on sharks because I think sharks are great. Some are big and some are small. Some are dangerous and some are not.
Did you know some sharks give birth to live babies and some lay eggs?
Wiggle your ear. Now wiggle the end of your nose. They move right? That's because they are made of cartilage, not bones. Did you know that sharks do not have one single bone in their bodies? Their skeleton is made up entirely of cartilage, just like in your ears and nose. Weird, eh? That's just one of the amazing shark facts you will be learning about today!
What if you were swimming in the warm blue sea and suddenly you saw a shark swimming toward you… Your dream has become a nightmare. What will you do?
Imagine standing at one end of a football field. Now someone is standing at the other end of the football field and they are talking to you. Do you think you could hear them? Well a shark can hear a fish moving in the water not just one but FIVE football fields away!
There are many different kinds of sharks in the world and I'm going to tell you about them now.

© 2014 *Nonfiction Writing Power* by Adrienne Gear. Pembroke Publishers. ISBN 978-1-55138-293-7

4 The Power to Describe

Descriptive writing is used when we want to share knowledge and facts about a particular topic. Sometimes this form of writing is known as *informational text*. While report writing is often considered to be a form of descriptive writing, sequence plays an important role in the retell; the order in which the writer shares information about a topic in descriptive writing is not as important. It is probably the form of nonfiction writing to which students in elementary school are most commonly exposed. This is likely due, in part, to the fact a high percentage of the nonfiction books in an elementary school library can be classified as descriptive. It is also fair to say that the traditional animal report is likely the most common form of nonfiction writing that is done in schools.

Overview of Descriptive Writing

DESCRIPTIVE WRITING AT A GLANCE

Purpose
- To share information and facts about a particular topic with the reader
- To give a general description: e.g., reports on animals, plants, machines, etc.
- To give a specific description: e.g., reports on a specific animal, plant, planet, etc.

Text Structure: What–What–What–What–What
1. **What** is your topic
2. **What**…
3. **What**…
4. **What**…
5. **What**…

Language Features
- Usually in third-person present tense
- Often includes technical vocabulary
- Action words: e.g., *run, explode, capture*
- Linking verbs: e.g., *as well, also, for one thing, is, are, belong to*
- Descriptive words: e.g., telling size, color, shape, texture
- Factual description
- Text features, such as diagrams, labels, webs, charts, maps

Examples
- Reports about various animals, countries, planets, insects, etc.
- Reports about specific animals, plants, insects, countries, etc.

Descriptive Anchor Books

Jim Arnosky, *All About Frogs* (P, I)
Nicola Davies, *Just Ducks* (P, I)
Deborah Hodge, *Ants* (I)
Deborah Hodge, *Bears* (I)
Deborah Hodge, *Bees* (I)
Martin Jenkins, *Ape* (P, I)
Steve Jenkins, *The Big Book of Beetles* (I)
Steve Jenkins, *Time to Eat* (series includes *Time to Bath, Time to Sleep*) (P)
Kate Riggs, *Cheetahs* (I)

Karen Wallace, *Gentle Giant Octopus* (P, I)
Jennifer Ward, *Somewhere in the Ocean* (P)
Jennifer Ward, *Forest Bright, Forest Night* (P)
Heinemann's My Life in the Wild series: *Life Cycle of a…* (series includes *Apple, Mushroom*) (P)
Heinemann's Seasons series: *Summer, Autumn, Winter, Spring* (P)
Heinnemann's Our Bodies series: *Our Bones, Our Brains, Our Blood* (P)

P = primary
I = intermediate
Note that book level is a suggestion only; all books can be used at any level. See page 23.

Intent

Rather than to retell a series of events, the intent of descriptive writing is to share information about a single topic with the reader. Connected subtopics provide details about the main topic. Descriptive writing often helps us classify and describe the way things are in the world. Writers give details about such general topics as animals, plants, insects, machines, countries, and celebrations; or they might choose to share information that focuses on a specific topic, such as tarantulas, Africa, grizzly bears, or praying mantises.

Form

Descriptive writing begins with a title and an opening that clearly identifies the topic. These are followed by facts on the topic, which are often grouped in paragraphs or under subheadings. Often a descriptive report will end with some form of summary.

The rhyme pattern developed to help students remember the form of descriptive writing sounds like this: What–What–What–What–What

Depending on the topic, *What* subtopics can be added.

1. *What* your topic is
2. *What:* subtopic 1
3. *What:* subtopic 2
4. *What:* subtopic 3
5. *What:* subtopic 4

Language Features

The following features are commonly found in descriptive writing:

- Written in simple present tense
- Verbs: action words (e.g., *run, explode, capture*)
- Linking verbs: *as well, also, for one thing, is, are, belong to, another*
- Adjectives: descriptive words telling about size, speed, color, shape, texture, etc.
- Signal words: *for example, specifically, such as, for instance, some, most, often*

Writing Techniques

Descriptive writing lends itself well to many lessons on writing techniques that enhance the style and form of the writing, and that enable the writer to ensure interesting and clear writing. The following writing techniques can be introduced as mini-lessons during your focus on desciptive writing:

- Nonfiction Text Features (see lesson on page 36)
- Interesting Details (see lesson on page 37)
- Triple-Scoop Words (see lesson on page 38)
- Organization (see lesson on page 43)
- Voice (see lesson on page 40)
- Introductions to Hook Your Reader (see lesson on page 42)

Links to Content Areas

Remember that descriptive report writing should not be restricted to writing about animals. There is a wide range of interesting topics linked to science and social studies that lend themselves very well to descriptive report writing.

Science	Social Studies
Plants/Trees: appearance, location, life cycle, needs, varieties	**Countries**: location, weather, people, land, food, government, culture/celebrations
Animals/Insects/Dinosaurs: appearance, behavior, food, habitat, enemies	**Peoples** (First Nations, pioneers, ancient civilizations): habitat, lifestyle, clothing, homes, food, tools, culture/beliefs, government
Planets: location in solar system, temperature, size, features, evolution	**Transportation**: origin, appearance, purpose, varieties, special features
Seasons: weather, Earth's rotation, changes to animals and plants	**Houses**: origin, inhabitants, location, structure, materials, features
Habitats: location, plant growth, animal life, land features	**Celebrations around the World**: origin, activities, time of year, foods
Focus on Animal Features: tails, wings, feet, etc.	**Famous Landmark or Structure**: location, origin, architecture, architect, special features

Assessment

This rubric can be used as a benchmark for assessing your students' descriptive writing. As always, I encourage you to make adjustments to the any of the comments to meet the needs of your specific grade.

DESCRIPTIVE WRITING ASSESSMENT RUBRIC

Title:	NY	M	FM	Ex
Form: Topic is clear; subtopics are clear and connected to topic.				
Organization: Facts are grouped together in paragraphs and/or under headings.				
Research: Student is able to locate information from books and nonbook sources.				
Writing: Student is able to interpret facts and express ideas in his/her own words.				
Style: Student is incorporating writing techniques, such as adding details, triple-scoop words, voice, and comparisons.				
Visuals: Writing includes nonfiction features effectively to support the text.				
Mechanics: Writing demonstrates effective use of spelling, punctuation, and grammar.				
***Wow!* Factor:** Writing shares information in a particularly interesting, unique, or surprising way.				

Introduction to Descriptive Writing

- Bring in several examples of descriptive books on a variety of topics: animals, insects, countries, plants, vehicles, planets, homes, etc. This should not be a problem as there will be a large collection in your library!
- Begin the lesson:

    Sometimes, a writer knows a lot of information about one thing. Or the writer is very interested in a topic and read to find out as much as he or she can about it. (Show the books and talk about the various topics.)
    These writers are like detectives, searching for facts. Once they collect and gather all the facts, they often want to share that information by writing it down for other people to read. This form of writing is called *descriptive* writing, because the writer is describing something. A writer might describe an animal, a season, a plant, a place, a country, a school. Writers sometimes focus on a topic like *bears* and describe different types of bears, or they might focus on one type of bear and describe that bear in detail.

- Explain that the skeleton of descriptive writing sounds like this: *What/What/ What/What/What.*

    After a writer chooses a topic to write about, he or she might ask him/herself: *What would my reader like to know about this topic?* The five *What*s are the five things the writer wants to tell the reader about the topic.

- Remind students that good writers always make a plan before they start to write. Explain that there are two ways to plan descriptive writing: creating a web plan or making a list plan.

  Both are great ways for writers to organize their ideas when they are going to describe something. Some people's brains work better using a web, while others work best with a list.

When modeling a plan for descriptive writing, I like to present both the web plan and list plan (see templates on pages 61 and 62) and allow students to choose the plan that works best for them.

- Model web planning:

  Let's say that I have decided I want to write about Grizzly Bears.
  (Write Grizzly Bears in the centre of chart paper)
  Now that I've decided on a topic, I need to ask myself "What would my reader like to know about Grizzly Bears?"
  (As students respond, add answers to the web: appearance, behavior, food, habitat, life cycle, enemies)

- Using the same topic and subtopics, do a second plan using the list form. Remind students that some writers prefer to use a list plan rather than a web.
- Continue the lesson:

  Once a writer has a plan, can he or she start writing?
  (No! They have to research and find facts for each part of the web.)
  Where would you find the facts?
  (Internet, books, etc.)
  Sometimes, writers spend a long, long time searching for the information and taking notes before they actually start writing. Why might a writer of fiction not need to do as much research as a nonfiction writer?
  (Because stories are often made up or based on the writer's experiences)

- Continue the lesson:

  Something that you might have noticed with many of the descriptive books we have looked at is that they have a lot of text features in them.

- Brainstorm a list of text features that you might see in a descriptive book: web, labels, captions, maps, charts, fact boxes, etc.
- Create an anchor chart for descriptive writing.

After attending an Orton Gillingham workshop for teachers, two colleagues of mine, Mary Cottrell and Jeanette Mumford, learned that web planning can be very confusing for children who have dyslexic tendencies. Offering students another option for planning has led to greater success in many students' writing.

Incorporating nonfiction text features can really help to enhance descriptive writing and make it more interesting. If your students have not been introduced to nonfiction text features, you might want to weave a few lessons from pages 17–18 into your study of descriptive writing.

> **Descriptive Writing Anchor Chart**
>
> - Includes a lot of information about one topic
> - Can be general (Bears) or specific (Grizzly Bears)
> - Includes a lot of facts, details, and examples
> - Has at least one *Wow!* fact
> - Includes nonfiction text features that represent the information in different ways
> - Uses these important words: *they*, *their*, *has*, *have*
> - Includes "some" or "most" statements

Whole-Class Write

Depending on the grade level, I recommend going through the process of writing a descriptive report as a whole class first, before students begin independent practice. This whole-class write provides an interactive way for you to model writing and can be linked to a unit you are focusing on in science or social studies. (For more on whole-class writes, see page 22.)

Interactive Plan

Note-taking is a required skill of all students. Whether they are searching the Internet, a magazine, or a book, students need to learn how to research, gather, and record key facts. Equally important is the need to learn to compose sentences that combine both the facts and their own words.

- Choose a topic for your whole-class write (connected, if possible, to a unit you are focusing on in science or social studies). Bring in a variety of leveled books on this topic.
- Begin the lesson:

  Yesterday we looked at the text structure for descriptive writing. Today, we are going to search for and collect facts and make a plan for our writing. I will be showing you two different ways to organize and record your facts onto a plan. These plans will help us when we go to do our writing later on.

- Write the word *Research* on the board. Ask students what it means. Ask them to find the small word (-*search*) in the big word. Circle or underline *search*.

  What does this word mean? (to look for, to find)
  What are we searching for when we research? (facts, information)
  What does "re-" mean? (If they are struggling, give another example such as "re-do" or "re-organize")
  It means "again"—so the word *research* means "to look for again."
  Why are we looking for it again? (because someone else already found the facts and wrote them down. We are now finding them again when we read).

- Explain that you will be working on a descriptive report as a class.

  Your job is to find facts about your topic. When you find a fact, you are to record it on your plan. These facts should be written in note form, not complete sentences. It's very important that you do not copy a sentence exactly; you have to put the idea in your own words.

- Model note-taking. Write the following sentences on the board:

  Bears are omnivores (which is a fancy way of saying they eat both meat and plants), just like people. They hunt animals, such as baby deer, caribou, and elk, but they are also scavengers, which means that they like leftovers, meat that other predators have left behind.

- Ask students on which arm of the web this information should be recorded. (food) Model how to add branches to the Food arm to record the facts (see student samples below). Repeat the same words on the list plan to show the difference.

These samples are by students in Grade 3.

Web Plan Sample

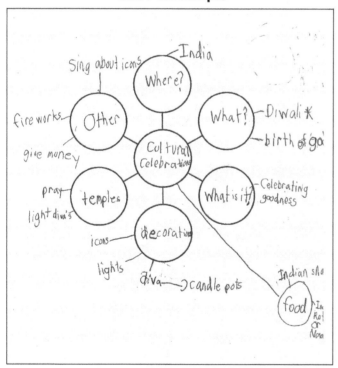

List Plan Sample

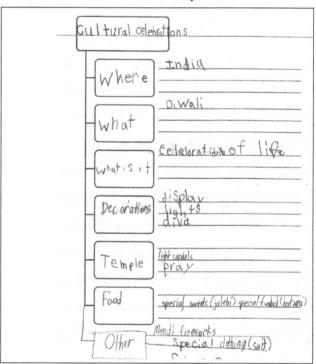

My catch phrase for taking notes is "Look for Mii in the book!" Mii stands for *Most important information.*

- Divide the class into groups and assign (or let them choose) one of the branches of the web to each group. In other words, each group has one *What* to research. *What* does a bear look like? *What* does a bear eat? *What* can a bear do (behavior)? *What* are the enemies of a bear? *What* is a bear's life cycle? *What* is a bear's habitat?
- Provide each group with a large chart paper and pen. Pass out books about bears and explain that each group is to find four or five facts on their topic. Remind students that they do not need to write full sentences, but use key words on their list or web.
- Provide time for groups to gather their facts and complete their plan.

Interactive Draft

There is a tendency for developing writers to turn a list of facts into a list of sentences. It is important that you take the time to model writing that is interesting and engaging. There are a number of important writing techniques that can be modelled over several days to help students develop engaging and interesting descriptions. See lessons on interesting details (page 37), triple-scoop words (page 38), and hooking your reader with a strong introduction (page 42).

- Once each group has gathered facts, bring the class together to model how to turn their facts into a paragraph.
- Provide time for groups to write a descriptive paragraph from their researched facts.
- Remind students that nonfiction features are an important addition to nonfiction descriptions because they help the reader understand the information in a different way. (If you have not introduced your class to nonfiction text features, see lesson on page 36).
- Brainstorm ways for students to add a nonfiction text features to support their paragraph. Invite students to think about a text feature they could include that could "show what they know" in a different way:

Sample Topics and Possible Text Features

- Appearance — diagram with labels (see student sample below)
- Behavior — fact box, caption
- Habitat — map and/or diagram with labels
- Food — web (see student sample below)
- Life cycle — flow chart
- Enemies — chart
- Interesting facts — fact box

The web sample (left) is by a student in Grade 3; the sample of a diagram with labels (right) is by a student in Grade 2.

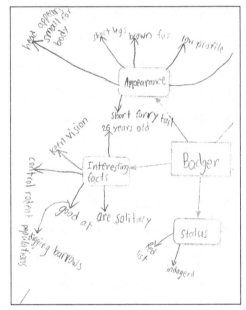
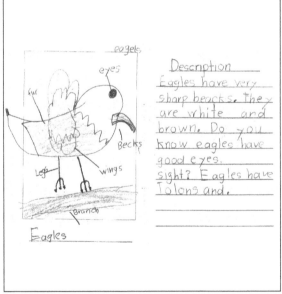

REVISING

Revision is an essential part of the writing process. Groups should have spent time reading their writing to ensure that it makes sense and that conventions have been edited. (See page 24 for more on revision.)

SHARING

Groups can present their information to the class. Depending on the grade level, the pages can be rewritten to create a class book.

Independent Write

When using the Description List Planner on page 62 with younger students, you can enlarge the template so they can draw inside the boxes, instead of writing.

Now that students have learned the structure and language of descriptive writing through the whole-class write, they are ready to choose their own topics for researching and writing. Once students have the selected their topic, it is important for them to complete the Description List Planner on page 62 or the Description Web Planner on page 61 before they begin their research. Students need to ask themselves "What do I think my reader would like to know about this topic?" This will help guide them to deciding on their five *What*s. Depending on the grade level, students might need support in determining the *What* headings for their research. Teachers of younger students might also choose to reduce the number of subtopics.

Allow several weeks for students to plan, research, write, and present their information, encouraging the use of both written texts and nonfiction features. Students can choose from a variety of formats to present their information, including mini-books, posters, and web pages.

Descriptive Writing Extension: ABC Books

Anchor Books

Varsha Bajaj, *T is for Taj Mahal: An India Alphabet* (P, I) (country)

James Foster, *S is for S'Mores – A Camping Alphabet Book* (P, I) (activity)

Beverly and Dereck Joubert, *African Animal Alphabet* (P) (animal)

Sonia Rodriguez, *T is for Tutu – A Ballet Alphabet Book* (P, I) (activity)

Melanie Ross, *Z is for Zamboni – A Hockey Alphabet Book* (P, I) (sport)

Mike Ulmer, *M is for Maple – A Canadian Alphabet Book* (P, I) (country)

P = primary
I = intermediate
Note that book level is a suggestion only; all books can be used at any level. See page 23.

I have a large collection of alphabet books. I enjoy how this simple format allows writers to explore a variety of topics in informative and often creative ways. Having students create alphabet books on a topic of their choice or that are connected to a content unit gives them a simple format that lends itself well to research and interesting descriptive writing. This lesson can be adapted to a wide range of grade levels and can vary from using a single word to a full paragraph to represent each letter of the alpahabet.

- Make a trip to your school or local library to collect a wide range of alphabet books to share.
- Provide students with the Alphabet Book Planning Page on page 63 to plan and gather facts.
- Students can transfer information from the Planning Page into a mini–alphabet-book format with accompanying illustrations.

Description Web Planner

Name: _____

(central circle connected by arrows to five surrounding ovals, each containing a blank line)

Description List Planner

Name: _____

Alphabet Book Planning Page

Name: _____ Topic: _____

Letter	Word	Sentence or Fact
A		
B		
C		
D		
E		
F		
G		
H		
I		
J		
K		
L		
M		
N		
O		
P		
Q		
R		
S		
T		
U		
V		
W		
X		
Y		
Z		

5 The Power to Instruct

Instructional texts are everywhere: they are the recipe books when we are cooking; the guide books when we are traveling; the instructions for a new video game; or the manuals when we are fixing our bike or putting together a piece of furntiture. There are sites for how to do just about anything you would want to learn. Instructional texts are practical, useful, and purposeful. Students are likely unaware of how often they are exposed to instructional texts in their day-to-day lives. The structure of this form of writing is relatively distinct and easy to recognize. It is also one that establishes a strong connection between writer and reader, as readers feel the writer is speaking directly to them. Once students become familiar with this text form, the possibilities of creatively incorporating it into content areas is endless!

Overview of Instructional Writing

INSTRUCTIONAL WRITING AT A GLANCE

Purpose
- To tell the reader how to achieve a particular goal
- To tell the reader how to follow a set of directions or procedures

Text Structure: What–What–How
1. **What** is being achieved
2. **What** you need (materials, ingredients or equipment)
3. **How** you do it (numbered steps, diagrams, illustrations, labels)
4. Optional: Tips and suggestions

Language Features
- Usually in second-person present tense: e.g., *you roll the dice; fold the paper*
- Action words connected to task: e.g., *put, let, stir, shake, kick, push, hold*
- Details of color, amount, size, time: e.g., *put in one cup; take the red square; squeeze a small amount; go through the big door*
- Details of how, when, and where: e.g., *cut carefully; after rolling the dice; two centimetres from the top*
- Transition words: e.g., *first, next, after that, finally*

Examples

Instructions on how to do a particular activity (recipes, games, crafts):
- How to make a fruit salad
- How to play checkers
- How to brush your teeth

Instructions that deal with human behavior:
- How to be healthy
- How to make your mom (dad, teacher) happy

- How to tie your shoelaces
- How to plant a seed
- How to make a make a paper airplane
- How to make a jam sandwich
- How to draw an apple
- How to wrap a present
- How to make a milkshake
- How to make your bed
- How to make a snowman
- How to change the batteries in your game player

- How to make a friend
- How to recycle
- How to help the Earth
- How to take care of your pet

Instructional Anchor Books

Lisa Brown, *How to Be* (P)
Nancy Carlson, *How To Lose All Your Friends* (P)
Lucy and Meg Clibbon, *Imagine You're A…* (series includes *Pirate, Wizard, Astronaut, Princess, Fairy*) (P, I)
Rebecca Doughty, *Some Tips for a Better World and a Happier Life* (P, I)
Neil Gaiman, *Instructions* (I)
Gail Gibbons, *My Soccer Book* (also similar books on baseball and football) (P)
Gail Gibbons, *How A House is Built* (P)
Jane G. Martel, *Smashed Potatoes* (P, I)
Meghan McCarthy, *The Astronaut Handbook* (P, I)

Nikki McClure, *How To Be A Cat* (P)
David Milgrim, *Eddie Gets Ready* (P)
Julie Morstad, *How To* (P, I)
Jenny Offill, *11 Experiments that Failed* (P, I)
Chris Raschka, *Everyone Can Learn to Ride a Bicycle* (P)
Susan Pearson, *How to Teach a Slug to Read* (P, I)
Scot Ritchie, *Look at That Building: A First Book of Structures* (P, I)
Melanie Walsh, *10 Things I Can Do to Help My World* (P)
Melanie Walsh, *My Green Day* (P)
Mélanie Watt, *Scaredy Squirrel* (any book) (P, I)

P = primary
I = intermediate
Note that book level is a suggestion only; all books can be used at any level. See page 23.

Intent

The intent of instructional writing, sometimes referred to as procedural writing, is tell the reader how to follow a set of procedures in order to make something, learn something, or achieve a particular goal. Instructional writing helps outline the specific steps the reader is required to follow and the equipment required, and often includes tips.

Form

Instructional writing is usually divided into three distinct parts: It begins with a clear statement of what is being achived in terms of a goal or aim; this is followed by a list of materials or equipment required; finally, the writer clearly outlines the specific steps the reader needs to follow in order to successfully achieve the goal. These steps are listed in order and might be numbered. Text features, such as illustrations, diagrams, and labels, are often used to help the reader follow the steps.

The rhyme pattern developed to help students remember the form of instructructions sounds like this: What–What–How

1. *What* is being achieved?
2. *What* are the items required?
3. *How* do you achieve this goal?

Language Features

The following are features commonly found in instructional writing:

- Action words connected to the task: e.g., *stir, shake, kick, cut, put*
- Details that give the reader specfic information about amount, color, size, time: e.g., *put in **one** teaspoon; take the **blue** ball; stir for **two** minutes; squeeze a **small** amount; stop at the **northwest corner***
- Details that give the reader specific details on how, when, or where: e.g., *cut **carefully**; **after** rolling the dice; **eight** centimetres from the top*
- Transition or sequence words: *first, then, next, finally*

Writing Technques

Instructional writing is very specific and requires the writer to provide clear, detailed, and sequential steps. While this form of writing does not lend itself to as many writing technques as some of the others in this book, there are some techniques that can be introduced or reviewed in mini-lessons during your focus on instructional writing:

- Nonfiction Features (see lesson on page 36)
- Interesting Details (see lesson on page 37)
- Organization (see lesson on page 43)

Links to Content Areas

Linking instructional writing to content areas provides students with an opportunity to practice the form, language, and intent with a wide range of topics. Here are some suggestions of ways to link instructional writing to your social studies or science topics:

Science	Social Studies
Plants/Trees: how to plant a seed; how to look after a plant	**Countries**: how to take a tour of Japan, Canada, etc.
Animals/Insects/Dinosaurs: how to be a… (animal, insect, dinosaur); how to take care of a pet	**Peoples**: different people, cultures, civilizations; survival guides or handbooks: e.g., how to be a Roman gladiator, a pioneer
Planets: how to get to Jupiter; how to survive on Mars	**Houses**: how to build an igloo
Seasons: how to dress in different seasons; how to build a snowman; how to spend the day at the beach	**First Nations**: how to make a totem pole; how to make Button Blanket; how to build a longhouse; how to plan a potlatch
Extreme Environment: how to survive on Mt. Everest, in the Marianas Trench, etc.	**Gold Rush**: how to pan for gold
Simple Machines: how to operate a ramp, pully, lever	**Celebrations around the World**: how to celebrate Divali, Christmas, Lunar New Year
Health: how to take care of yourself; how to exercise; how to eat healthily; recipes for healthy snacks	**Famous Landmark or Structure**: how to build the Great Wall of China, Stonehenge, the Eiffel Tower

	Mapping: how to get from point A to point B (my house to the school, the office to the library)

Assessment

This rubric can be used as a benchmark for assessing your students' instructional writing. As always, I encourage you to make adjustments to the any of the comments to meet the needs of your specific grade.

INSTRUCTIONAL WRITING ASSESSMENT RUBRIC

NY = Not Yet Meeting expectations
M = Meeting expectations (minimum level)
FM = Fully Meeting expectations
Ex = Exceeding expectations

Title:	NY	M	FM	Ex
Form: Topic is clear; writing demonstrates the What–What–How structure.				
Organization: Clear, sequential instructions are given.				
Meaning: Includes specific details that support the steps.				
Style: Uses appropriate action and transition words.				
Visuals: Includes nonfiction features effectively to support the text.				
Mechanics: Demonstrates effective use of spelling, punctuation, and grammar.				

Introduction to Instructional Writing

Having fun by following instructions that your students write is a great way of generating their interest in the form and teaching them the importance of clarity. This introductory lesson is one that always creates a lot of laughter and a bit of mess (bring a towel!).

To help make this lesson succeed, try not to provide very much instruction about instruction.

- Begin the lesson:

    Today we are going to start investigating another form of nonfiction writing. We will start with a little activtiy that will help you understand the skeleton of this type of writing. I want you to imagine that an extraterrestrial alien is a visitor in your house. This alien is learning the ways of Earthlings and you are teaching it some of your day-to-day routines. Today you are going to teach it how to brush your teeth. On this piece of paper, I would like you to write the information the alien would need to follow in order to brush his or her teeth.

- Pass out paper and allow time for students to write. While they are writing, walk around and take note of students who are not providing clear instructions: these are the examples you will be using!
- Collect the papers and take a few minutes to select the two or three examples that you know are the least helpful. Bring students together and explain that

you have selected some papers that you will read out loud and then use to brush your teeth. Remind students that you are the alien and you have no idea how to brush your teeth apart from what they have written.

- Using a cup of water, a toothbrush, and toothpaste (floss optional), begin to follow the instructions exactly as written: e.g., if student has written "put toothpaste on toothbrush," put the contents of the whole tube on the wrong end of the brush. Feel free to get a little silly when interpreting the instructions! Imagine how easy it would be to misinterpret instructions like these, written by a Grade 3 student:

  Instructions for Brushing Your Teeth
  - Take a toothbrush and put the toothpaste on top.
  - Put it in your mouth and move your arm up and down.
  - Get the ones at the back and spit.
  - Go up and down and spit again.
  - If you want you can floss.

To help students remember Sequence–Action–Detail as the important components of instructional writing, I tell them to think of the acronym SAD, because sad is what readers will be if they are unable to follow the instructions!

- Students will begin to laugh and shout "No!" Reply, "But that's what it says to do!"
- After the demonstration, reflect on the lesson. Explain that this form of nonfiction writing is called instruction. Ask students what would be the purpose of writing instructions for someone to read. (to tell the reader how to do an activity or to achieve something)
- Ask students what the demonstration taught them. (the importance of providing clear, sequential instructions; the importance of including specific details)
- Brainstorm different kinds of instructions students might be familiar with. Begin with the words *How to...*: e.g., play a new video game, do a puzzle, fix a bike, cook, draw a cartoon, build something, lose weight, get fit.
- Explain that the skeleton of instructional writing sounds like this: What–What–How. They build instructions on **What** the task or goal is/**What** materials you need/**How** you do it. Using the What–What–How structure, model how to improve on the instructions they just wrote; see sample below). Invite class to help you.

Teacher Model

Smashed Potatoes by Jane G. Martel is a hilarious collection of recipes written by students who clearly had no instruction on writing instructions! It is a fun read-aloud and a would be a great complement to this lesson.

> **What:** *How to brush your teeth*
> **What:** *Toothbrush, toothpaste, water*
> **How:** *First, squeeze a small amount of toothpaste onto the bristles of the toothbrush.*
> *Next, wet the toothbrush with water.*
> *Then, put the brush end of the toothbrush in your mouth.*
> *Next, move the brush up and down along your top teeth.*
> *Repeat brushing on the bottom teeth.*
> *After you are finished, spit toothpaste into the sink.*
> *Finally, rinse your mouth with water and SMILE!*

- You may choose to have your students rewrite their instructions following the What–What–How format.

Features of Instructional Writing

Before launching into instructional writing lessons with your class, it is important to spend some time focusing on the key features: second-person point of view, action words, transition words, and text features. Depending on the grade level, you might want to divide this lesson into two shorter ones.

- Begin the lesson:

    I'd like to spend some time today looking at some important features of instructional texts. Every form of writing has a few important key features that make it unique from other forms of writing. We learned yesterday that the skeleton of instruction follows the What–What–How structure. Today we are going to look at the important features.

FEATURE 1: WRITING IN THE SECOND PERSON

- Write the following sentences on the board:

    1. *I brush my teeth.*
    2. *You brush your teeth.*
    3. *He brushes his teeth.*

- Ask students what is different about these sentences. (the point of view of the writer) Explain:

    Sentence 1 is written in what is called *first* person—the writer is talking about him/herself.
    Sentence 2 is written in *second* person—the writer is talking to the reader or telling the reader to do something.
    Sentence 3 is written in *third* person—the writer is writing about something that is happening to someone else, as if watching it happen, and telling the reader about it.

I like to tell children that when you write instructions you get to "be the boss" and order people to do exactly what you want them to do. And you don't even say "please"!

- Ask students which sentence they think would be the best sentence to use for instructions. (sentence 2, because it sounds as if the writer is giving the reader instructions) Explain that instructional text is always written in second-person point of you. To emphasize this point, give an example of a sentence from a recipe book turned into a third-person statement:

    Beat the eggs until fluffy.
    OR
    She beats the eggs until they are fluffy.
    (The second example would sound very funny if it were written in a recipe!)

FEATURE 2: TRANSITION WORDS

- Write the following words on the board: *first, second, next, third, then, afterward, later, finally, before*
- Ask students what they notice about the words. (They are all words that explain order or sequence.)
- Tell students that these are called *transition words*—words that help the reader move from one step to the next step.
- Ask why these are important signal or cue words for instructional texts. (because they help organize the steps in the correct order for the reader)

- Explain that sometimes a writer uses numbers instead of words to show the order of steps, or that a writer might use both numbers and transition words.
- Refer back to your How to Brush Your Teeth model (see page 68) and underline the first word in each sentence to show students transition words being used in instructions.

FEATURE 3: ACTION WORDS

- Refer back to your How to Brush Your Teeth model (see page 68). Draw the students' attention to the How sentences.
- Underline the second word in each sentence and ask students what they notice. (Every word is a verb or action word.)
- Explain that another key feature of instructional text is that the writer uses very clear action words, or verbs, to help the reader understand what to do. Tell students that when they write instructions, it is important to include an action word in each step. Action words will be different, depending on what the instructions are for.
- Brainstorm some action words for different instructions:

  Action words for baking: *roll, stir, chop, mix*
  Action words for riding a bike: *push, pedal, look*
  Action words for playing a board game: *roll, move, choose, start, finish*

FEATURE 4: NONFICTION FEATURES

Students will need to have had some practice with nonfiction features prior to this lesson. See lesson on page 36.

- Choose an anchor book: a children's cookbook that uses visuals to support instructions; LEGO instructions.
- Remind students that nonfiction writing is often accompanied by visuals called nonfiction features. Nonfiction features help the reader understand the information more clearly.
- Brainstorm a list of nonfiction features: fact boxes, labels, photographs, captions, tables, maps, webs.
- Ask students if they think nonfiction features would be helpful in instructional writing. How? (to label things; to show what something looks like; to show visuals for steps)
- Show examples from anchor books of how different instructional texts use visuals.

The popular Scaredy Squirrel books by Mélanie Watt, although fiction in context, are excellent examples of how to use text features to enhance instructions.

- Introduce the concept of *tips* as an added feature for instructional texts. Explain that often a writer will include some helpful tips to help their reader be successful. Ask students what tips they might include for How to Brush Your Teeth. (Make sure to brush for 3 minutes; Don't squeeze too much toothpaste; Remember to rinse.) Explain that tips often begin with these words: *Always, Never, Don't, Be sure to, Try to, Be careful not to, Remember to.*

Have students help you create an anchor chart for Instructional Writing.

Instructional Writing

- Follows the What–What–How text structure
- Is written in second person (Be the boss!)
- Uses action words
- Uses transition words or numbers
- Includes text features to help the reader
- Sometimes includes tips

Whole-Class Write

How to Make or Build Something

While instructional writing does not require extensive modeling lessons, it is important to work through one interactive lesson where you are modeling the writing on an interactive whiteboard or chart stand with assistance from your students.

Anchor Books

Maxine Anderson, *Leonardo da Vinci Inventions You Can Build Yourself* (Build it Yourself series) (I)
Annabell Carmel, *Mom and Me Cookbook* (P)
Betty Crocker, *Betty Crocker Kids Cook!* (P, I)
Gail Gibbons, *How a House is Built* (P, I)
Deborah Hopkins, *How They Built the Empire State Building* (I)
Carol A. Johmann, *Bridges: Amazing Structures to Design, Build and Test* (I)

Jennifer L. Marks, *How to Make a Bouncing Egg* (P)
Erica Shores, *How to Make Bubbles* (P)
Lori Shores, *How to Build Fizzy Rocket* (P)
Lori Shores, *How to Make Slime* (P)
Linda White, *Cooking on a Stick: Campfire Recipes for Kids* (P, I)
Roxanne Ladczack Williams, *How to Make a Mudpie* (P, I)
Valerie Wyatt, *How to Build your Own Country* (I)

P = primary
I = intermediate
Note that book level is a suggestion only; all books can be used at any level. See page 23.

- Begin the lesson:

  We have been talking about instructional writing. There are many different kinds of instructions that writers give their readers. I brought in a few different books for us to look through.

- Divide the class into small groups and give each group a few books. If possible, give each group at least one recipe book, one craft book, and one book on how to create or build something.
- Invite students to look through the books and see if they can identify the writer's intent (see page 32) and the What–What–How text structure.
- Bring students together to discuss what the books had in common. (All gave instructions on how to make, create, or build something.)

Recipes are a great way for children to learn instructional writing, especially if you do cooking or baking activities in your classroom. Robyn Fenyedi, a Kindergarten teacher at General Wolfe Elementary in Vancouver, uses her monthly cooking class to help her students learn the transition words of instructions.

- Explain that today they are going to be writing instructions on how to make something. Remind the students they will need to follow the What–What–How structure and to use action and transition words.
- Write *How to Make a Tuna Sandwich* on chart paper or the interactive whiteboard.
- Ask students to think of some action words connected to the topic: *open, mix, spread, cut.*
- Review:

  > *What* is my intent? To tell my reader *how* to make a tuna sandwich.
  > *What* do I need? Bread, lettuce, mayo, can of tuna, knife. (Explain that they could draw little pictures of the ingredients and label them.)
  > *How* do I make it? (Remind the students to use transition words and action words.)

- Invite students to help you with the steps, recording as you go.

  > First, **open** tuna can (sketch a picture of tuna can and opener; label)
  > Next, **drain** tuna (sketch tuna can tipped with liquid coming out; include arrow)
  > Then, **put** tuna in a bowl.
  > Next, **add** a spoonful of mayonnaise.
  > After that, **mix** tuna and mayo until smooth.
  > Next, **spread** tuna mixture on a slice of bread.
  > Next, **add** 2 leaves of washed lettuce on top of tuna mixture.
  > Then, **cover** with another slice of bread.
  > Finally, **cut** sandwich in half and serve.

- Remind students that sometimes writers include tips to help their readers avoid mistakes. Ask what tip they might give for making the sandwich taste great. (Use fresh bread for a better taste! Buy tuna packed in water instead of oil. Add chopped onions or celery for crunch.)
- Ask if there are any other text features that could be added? (nutrition chart, pictures, labels)
- Students should now be ready to write their own instructions for how to make something. Brainstorm a list of possible topics. Encourage students to choose a topic with which they are already familiar. I recommend focusing on smaller tasks to reduce complicated steps. Here are some suggestions for topics:

Teach your students the difference between a *fact box* and a *tip box*. Tips are often included in instructions, whereas fact boxes are often added to descriptions.

  - How to make a snowman
  - How to make a paper airplane
  - How to make s'mores
  - How to make cookies
  - How to cook rice
  - How to make a sandwich
  - How to make chocolate milk
  - How to make your bed
  - How to make a smoothie
  - How to make a house of cards

- Once students have decided on a topic, invite them to share their topic and at least four action words connected to their topic with a partner before they start to write.

- Pass out a How-To planning page and allow time for students to complete their instructions. There are three planner pages to choose from: Planner 1 on page 84 is designed for intermediate students; Planner 2 on pages 85–86 (the two pages should be copied back-to-back or side by side on larger paper; see student sample below) is designed for primary students; Planner 3 on page 87 is designed for Kindergarten students. Of course, you are welcome to use any planner with any grade. For younger students, I recommend enlarging these pages to give them more space to write.

These samples are by students in Grade 3.

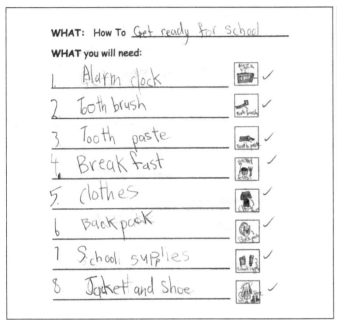

Independent Write

Instructions for an Activity or Skill

Anchor Books

Let's Play Soccer (DK Readers) (P, I)
Jason Carter Eaton, *How to Train a Train* (P, I)
Peer Eldin, *The Most Excellent Book of How to Be a Magician* (series includes clown and cheerleader) (I)
Mark Evans, *Fish* (ASPCA Pet Care Guides for Kids; series includes hamsters, kittens, puppies, bunnies) (P)
John Frank, *How to Catch a Fish* (P, I)
Mordicai Gerstein, *How to Bicycle to the Moon to Plant Sunflowers* (P, I)
Gail Gibbons, *My Soccer Book* (P)
Gail Gibbons, *My Baseball Book* (P)

Gail Gibbons, *My Football Book* (P)
Sally Lloyd Jones, *How to Get a Job – by Me, the Boss* (P, I)
Sally Lloyd Jones, *How to Get Married – by Me, the Bride* (P, I)
David Milgrim, *Eddie Gets Ready for School* (P)
Susan Pearson, *How to Teach a Slug to Read* (P, I)
Chris Raschka, *Everyone Can Learn to Ride a Bicycle* (P, I)
Jean Reagan, *How to Babysit Grandpa* (P, I)
Vera Williams, *Three Days on a River in a Red Canoe* (I)

P = primary
I = intermediate
Note that book level is a suggestion only; all books can be used at any level. See page 23.

- Gather a collection of instructional texts that focus on how to do something (see list of anchor books). Invite students to look through the books and pay attention to the writer's intent and the What–What–How text structure.

- Introduce a topic involving an activity or skill: e.g., *How to get ready for school*; *How to take care of your pet*; *How to play a sport*. (For the purpose of modeling, focus on one topic only.)
- Ask students to think about some of the things involved in the activity you've chosen. Invite them to share in partners and encourage them to use transition words when they are sharing: *first*, *next*, *then*, etc. Brainstorm a list of things you might need and a list of action words that might be included.
- Discuss possible tips for success in the activity. Ask students which text features could be included. Encourage them to think about tips they could add.
- Using How-To Planner 1 (page 84), 2 (pages 85–86), or 3 (page 87), students complete their own set of instructions.
- For further practice in writing instructions, invite students to chose their own topic. Encourage them to chose small, manageable topics and brainstorm action words (verbs) beforehand. Here are some more suggestions for possible topics:

  - How to get ready for bed
  - How to play soccer/hockey
  - How to do gymnastics/go swimming
  - How to throw a party
  - How to make your bed
  - How to ride a bike
  - How to drink from a water fountain
  - How to dive into a pool
  - How to tie your shoes
  - How to wash your dog

Instructions for Getting Somewhere

- Draw a bird's eye view of your classroom: label such things as door, window(s), teacher's desk, carpet area, computer area, etc. Photocopy a class set of maps onto the Classroom Directions template on page 88.
- Reproduce the map in a larger format on a chart stand or project it with a document camera. On the larger map, draw a pathway with arrows from the doorway to a desk. To make it more interesting, use a slightly indirect route; see sample below.

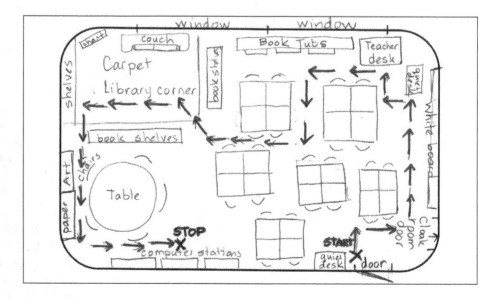

- Begin the lesson:

    We have been focusing on writing instructions. We have learned about instructions for making something and for doing something. Today we are going to learn about another type of instructions.

- Show students the classroom map and ask what kind of instructions would be used with a map. (directions) Ask students what a writer's intent is when writing directions. (helping the reader get somewhere) Ask what action words would be important when writing directions (*start, turn, go straight, left, right, stop*)
- Tell students to look at the map and think about how they would give instructions to follow the route on the map. Give students time to think and practice.
- Ask one student to think about the first instruction, then another student to think of the next. As each student gives you directions, physically follow their instructions and move around the room.
- As a class, reflect on some of the challenges and important things to remember.
- Model how you would write these directions clearly for someone to follow. Remind students the importance of the words *START* and *END*, and that other important action words for directions might be *go*, *walk*, *turn*, *straight*, *left*, *right*.

Teacher Model

  - *Start at the classroom door.*
  - *First, walk straight until you get to the table.*
  - *Then stop.*
  - *Next, turn left.*
  - *Finally, walk toward the computer centre.*

- Hand out classroom maps to students. Explain that they will be drawing a route from one place in the classroom to another. After they draw the route on the map, they will be writing the directions for the route they have drawn. Explain that the more complicated the route is, the more steps they will need to write
- After students have completed drawing their routes and writing their directions, invite them to find a partner to test out their directions. One student reads the directions aloud to his/her partner. If the partner ends up going the wrong way, the mapper knows there is a need to make some adjustments.

LESSON EXTENSIONS

School Directions
Students expand this lesson to directions within the school; for example, how to get from my classroom to the office; how to get to the library from my classroom. Students will need to actually take the route to know the specific steps. I find this lesson works well if the students are working in pairs.

Neighborhood Directions
Students can, with the help of their parents, make an accurate map with directions of how to get from home to school. Street names and number of blocks would be important to include.

Map Directions

Students can create an imaginary map of an island; see Island Map Directions on page 89. They can plan their island around a theme, such as Candy Island, Flower Island, Playground Island, Rainbow Island. Remind them of things to include on the island:

- Arrival and departure location; e.g., dock, airport
- 5–6 landmarks; e.g., forest, mountain, store, rollercoaster, river, lake, waterfall, market, hotel
- roads that lead to each landmark
- a compass rose and key (optional)

This sample is by a student in Grade 3.

After students have completed their maps, they write instructions on how to spend the day on their island.

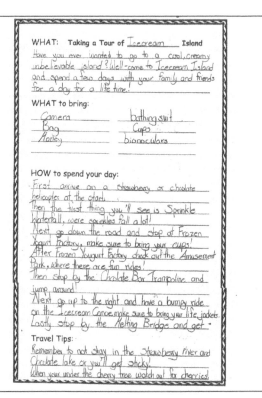

Instructions for Self-Improvement or Making the World Better

Anchor Books

Laurie Krasny Brown, *How to Be A Friend* (P, I)
Nancy Carlson, *How to Lose All Your Friends* (P, I)
Rebecca Doughty, *Some Tips for a Better World and a Happier Life* (P, I)
Charlotte Guillain, *Saving Water* (Helping the Environment series, ACORN) (P)

Barbara Joose, *Please is a Good Word to Say* (P, I)
Paul Mason, *Caring for Critters* (P)
Melanie Walsh, *10 Things I Can Do to Help My World* (P)
Melanie Walsh, *My Green Day* (P)

P = primary
I = intermediate

- Begin the lesson:

  Sometimes, writers use instructions to help people improve themselves. Sometimes these are called *self-help* books because they are helping you improve yourself. Can you think of some examples of this kind of book? (how to lose weight, get rich, quit smoking, exercise, be grateful) Other times, a writer might write instructions for a reader who wants to do something to help the world or others. Can you think of some examples? (how to live and eat green; how to build a school in Africa; how to recycle; how to help in your community; how to volunteer; how to think locally, not globally; how to make friends)

- Explain that today they are going to choose a topic for giving instructions on improving either themselves or the world.
- Share any of the anchor books. Ask students if they think the book is for readers to improve themselves or improve the world.
- Explain that they will be chosing a topic for writing instructions for readers to improve themselves or improve the world.
- Invite students to offer suggestions on how to help at home. Brainstorm a list of tasks:

  - Clean room
  - Do homework
  - Take out garbage
  - Pick up dog poop
  - Help with dishes

- Explain that writers can add details to their lists to make them more interesting for their readers. This is also a way of incorporating voice into instructions. Model examples:

  - *Put dirty clothes in the laundry basket (not on the floor!).*
  - *Rinse the toothpaste spit off the sink (dry toothpaste is hard to clean!).*
  - *Put your dirty dishes in the dishwasher (not on the counter!).*
  - *Offering your help—"Can I help you Mom?"—will make your mom very happy!*
  - *Say "thank-you" to your parents every day. Those two words mean a lot!*

- Model how to invite readers in by clearly stating the importance of these instructions.

  Moms and dads work hard to help you every day. Helping them at home can make them feel great and can make you feel great too! Here are a few things you can do to help make your parents life just a little easier:

- Brainstorm some possible topics for students to write about:

  How to Be Healthy
  How Make/Keep Your Friends
  How to Demonstrate Good Behavior at Home/at School/at the Movies
  How to Be Polite
  How to Be Helpful at Home/at School
  How to be a Good Sister/Brother

Nancy Carlon's book *How to Lose All Your Friends* is written in the negative, which makes for an unusual and humorous look at instructions. (One of my students described it as being written "backwards"!) Primary teacher Cheryl Burian reads *How to Lose All Your Friends* at the start of every year and has her students write a list of instructions on How to Keep All Your Friends.

Teacher Model

How to Help Your School Be Green
How to Be Green
How to Live a Happy Life
How to Take Care of your Pet
How to Keep your School Clean
How to Take Care of your Neighborhood

Once students have decided on a topic, they can begin to write. Remind students to begin with an opening statement that invites their readers in, to include interesting details, and to include action words.

Melanie Silverson, primary teacher in Richmond, BC, ends her school year by inviting her students to write instructions on How to Drive Your Teacher Coconuts. What fun her Grade 3 students have with this writing lesson!

How to Drive Your Teacher Coconuts
(and bananas)

Listening at the carpet

1. At the carpet play hand games, play with your hair and play with your shoe laces.

2 Sit on the carpet looking out the Window at the cloud shapes day dreaming.

3. Talk to your best friend when the teacher is teaching.

4. Distract other people from learning by acting silly

How to Be Me

Anchor Books

Judy Allan, Backyard Books series (P, I)   Joanne Ryder, *Snail's Spell* (P, I)
Lisa Brown, *How to Be* (P, I)

P = primary
I = intermediate

Teacher Model

• Write a short description of yourself on the board or interactive whiteboard.

My name is Ms Gear. I am a teacher at J.W. Sexsmith school in Vancouver. I am married to Richard and we have two children—Spencer and Oliver. We have a dog named Bailey. I have written three books for teachers. I love reading books and gardening and skiing with my family.

• Read your description aloud and ask students what your intent was for this piece. (to describe yourself; to tell the reader about yourself) Explain that this writing is called *descriptive* because it is describing a topic.
• Read aloud *How to Be* by Lisa Brown.

The idea of writing How to Be Me poems comes from *Nonfiction Mentor Texts* by Lynne R. Dorfman & Rose Cappelli (Stenhouse, 2009).

- Ask students what they noticed about the writing. (instructional writing; started sentences with action words or verbs) How was it different from your description? (written as intructions)
- Ask students what the writer's intent was. (to share characteristics of the animals with the reader through instructions; to let the reader actually feel what it would be like to be that animal) Ask what the author needed to do before writing the book? (research characteristics about the animal)
- Explain that they are going to write instructions for How to Be Me.

  The intent is to provide the reader with a set of instructions on how to be you. This piece of writing will be very easy to do because you are experts about yourselves. What would a reader need to know if they were going to try to be you? (what you are like; your likes and dislikes; your talents, interests, hobbies)

- Hand out copies of the How-to-Be-_____ Planning Page from page 90. Model the page with the students using a think-aloud:

Teacher Model

HOW TO BE MS GEAR

Equipment	Physical Skills
• my family	• Run
• my dog	• Read
• friends	• Write
• books	• Bake
• my car	• Garden
• Christmas decorations	• Ski
• red licorice	• Listen
• laptop	• Carry groceries
• gardening shovel	• Cook
• music	• Drive
• my bed	• Laugh
Personality Traits	**Tips from the Expert**
• Friendly	• Love your family most of all
• Determined	• Read lots of books
• Funny	• Laugh a lot
• Kind	• Never give up
• Passionate	• Sniff new books
	• Sing very loudly in the car
	• Cry at the singing of the national anthem
	• Appreciate the 4 seasons
	• Spend lots of time in your garden

- Explain that the *skills* (action words) should try to match the *equipment*; e.g., *books – read; family – love.*
- Remind students that tips usually start with the words *sometimes, always, never, don't, remember, try, be sure to.*
- Provide students time to complete the four boxes of the Planner.
- After students have completed their templates, model how to turn their lists into instructions (see Teacher Model).
- Remind students that they need to start each line with an action word (verb).

- Encourage students to include personal details that nobody else would have, rather than general ones like *get up, eat breakfast, go to school*, etc.

Teacher Model

How to be Ms Gear

Love everything but love your family most of all
Live each day to the fullest
Laugh a lot
Cry during the national anthem
Eat too much red licorice at a movie theatre
Be amazed by the beauty of the changing seasons
Drive to many ballparks and hockey rinks
Cheer loudly when watching your children play sports
Hide in bathrooms when your son is playing in goal
Lose your keys at least once a week
Try your best all the time
Bring your writer's notebook everywhere, just in case
Read lots and lots and lots of books
Bake cookies and muffins
Write books about reading and writing for teachers
Dream of writing a children's book
Sniff new books in the bookstore
Make lots of lists and lose some of them
Love your job and feel blessed that you love it so much
Wear long sweaters and boots
Be grateful, passionate, and kind.

The How to Be Me sample (left) is by a student in Grade 3; the How to Be an Animal sample (right) is by a student in Grade 4.

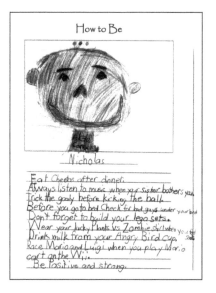

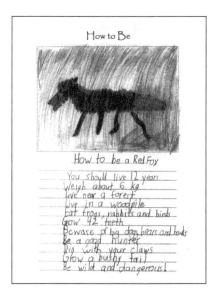

How to Be an Animal

Younger students can use animal facts to write a How to Be an Animal poem. Or they can create a mini-book, with one instruction and an illustration per page.

Following the lesson on How to Be Me, students will be able to use their knowledge to write a how-to-be piece about an animal of their choice. Researching behavior, appearance, and unique features of an animal and combining it with instructional writing makes for a worthwhile and engaging exercise. Students will choose an animal (or insect, bird, or reptile) and will write instructions on how to become that animal. Before writing, however, they will need to become experts by gathering facts about their animal.

- Begin the lesson:

  We have written How to Be Me instructions. Now we will be writing instructions again, except we will be focusing on an animal instead of ourselves. We will be doing some research to gather some facts in help us with our writing.

- Invite students to read the Racoon samples on page 91. Ask them what they noticed about the writing. (Sample 1 is a description; Sample 2 is instructions.)
- Invite students to choose an animal, insect, or bird they would like to focus on.
- Pass out the How-to-Be-an-Animal Planner (page 92).
- Allow several periods of research time for them to gather facts about their animals.

If you have a copy of *How to Be* by Lisa Brown, read it aloud and invite students to listen to how the writer used instructions to share facts about the animals.

- Once students have completed their fact sheets, model how to turn a fact into instructions by starting with action words. Invite students to help you.

Fact	$\longrightarrow$	Instruction
Eagles are large, powerful birds of prey.	$\longrightarrow$	Be a powerful hunter.
Eagles have large, hooked beaks.	$\longrightarrow$	Use your large, hooked beak to catch your prey.
Eagles have excellent eyesight.	$\longrightarrow$	Use your excellent eyesight to spot your prey.

- Remind students that their intent is to teach their reader interesting information about their animal through instructions.

Lesson Extensions

HOW TO BE AN EXPERT

These lessons provide an excellent opportunity to link instructional writing with science and social studies content.

Using the same format as How to Be Me writing, students can create How to Be poems about something they are experts in.

- Brainstorm activities they are involved in or know a lot about: e.g., hockey, soccer, baseball, football, karate, ballet, swimming, yo-yo, bird watching, piano, violin.
- Have students use the template from page 90; however, this time, the students will be focusing on one skill or hobby to give instructions about.

Crofton House teacher Stephanie Yorath invited her Grade 1 students to write expert books.

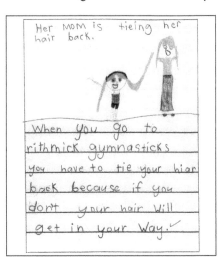

Anchor Books

Marla Frazee, *Walk On: A Guide for Babies of All Ages* (P, I)

Meghan McCarthy, *Astronaut Handbook* (P, I)

P = primary
I = intermediate
Note that book level is a suggestion only; all books can be used at any level. See page 23.

There are many ways you can use the How to Be framework of instructional writing to link to content areas. Depending on grade level and area of study, these writing lessons could link to the study of real people in either science or social studies as an alternative to writing biographies. Students would, of course, need to spend time researching facts about the person to acquire the necessary background information. Here are some examples:

- How to Be People in a Family: e.g., mother, father, brother, sister, baby, grandma
- How to Be People in the Community: e.g., police officer, teacher, post-office worker, garbage collector, mayor, bus driver, fireman
- How to Be People Connected to Natural Resources: e.g., forester, fisher, farmer, orchardist, logger, miner
- How to Be an Athlete: e.g., soccer player, hockey goalie, baseball player
- How to Be a Famous Person: e.g., Terry Fox, Andy Murray, Chris Hadfield, Justin Bieber, Barack Obama
- How to Be People in History (general): e.g., a Neanderthal, Roman gladiator, Egptian queen, peasant, pioneer, explorer, king or queen, president or prime minister
- How to Be People in History (specific): King Charles I, Caesar, Napoleon, Joan of Arc, Marie Antoinette, Christopher Columbus, Isaac Newton, Galileo, Thomas Edison, Michelangelo, Mother Teresa, Abraham Lincoln, Martin Luther King, Terry Fox, Sir John A. Macdonald, Jacques Cartier

Instructional Writing Extension: Survival Guides or Handbooks

Anchor Books

Anna Claybourne, *Treasure Hunter's Handbook* (P, I)
Anna Claybourne, *Go Greek* (P, I)
Anna Claybourne, *Coastal Treasure Hunter* (P, I)
Anna Claybourne, *A Roman Soldier's Handbook* (P, I)
Lucy and Meg Clibbon, *How to Be…* series (includes *Knight, Astronaut, Pirate, Princess, Fairy*, etc.) (P, I)

Lisa Kopelke, *Younger Brother's Survival Guide* (P, I)
Meghan McCarthy, *Astronaut Handbook* (P, I)
Helena McShane, *Oliver in Vancouver* (P, I)

P = primary
I = intermediate
Note that book level is a suggestion only; all books can be used at any level. See page 23.

Applying students' knowledge of instructional writing to create guidebooks or handbooks can be another way to integrate content and writing in an exciting format. Students' previous knowledge of nonfiction features, voice, humor, and facts and tips can be applied together in one larger writing project. Students will enjoy becoming experts and sharing their knowledge in this interesting format.

It is important for students to first understand the purpose and format of a handbook or guidebook. If possible, bring in samples to share with your students. Explain that the purpose of a guidebook is to give readers instructions on a specific place or time, and that a handbook is to provide instructions about people or positions. Both provide the reader with a lot of instructions, advice, and tips about one subject.

Some guidebooks are to help readers become familiar with a new city when they are traveling. Brainstorm some travel tips that might be included: e.g., best places to eat, transportation advice, top sightseeing spots, hotels, do's and don't's of the culture, etc. Guidebook writing projects can be integrated into a study of a place or a particular time period or culture.

Handbooks instruct readers on what it means to be a particular type of person or have a particular job or position. Here are just a few examples;

- pioneer handbook
- medieval handbook
- early human handbook (Neanderthal)
- peasant handbook
- First Nations handbook
- explorer handbook
- knight handbook
- ancient Greek/Rome/Eygptian handbook
- gladiator handbook
- samurai handbook

Students might find the Handbook Planning Page (page 93) a useful way to organize their information.

Provide students with mini-books to create their guide/handbooks. Remind them of the importance of using text features to present their information and that they should make every effort to use instructional form and language in their books.

How-To Planner 1

Name: _____

How to _____

What you will need:

How:

1. _____

_____

2. _____

_____

3. _____

_____

4. _____

_____

5. _____

_____

6. _____

_____

TIP: _____

How-To Planner 2: page 1

Name: _____

WHAT: How To _____

WHAT you will need:

_____

_____

_____

_____

_____

_____

How-To Planner 2: page 2

HOW to _____

1 _____ _____ _____	**2** _____ _____ _____	**3** _____ _____ _____
4 _____ _____ _____	**5** _____ _____ _____	**6** _____ _____ _____

How-To Planner 3

Name: _____

How to _____

First…	Next…
Then…	Finally…

Classroom Directions

Name: _____

┌───┐
│   │
│   │
│   │
│   │
│   Place map of classroom here   │
│   │
│   │
│   │
│   │
└───┘

How to get from _____ to _____

_____

_____

_____

_____

_____

Island Map Directions

Name: _____

Some direction words you might need:

Start	*Continue*	*Don't*
Visit	*Turn left*	*Go until you see/reach*
Enjoy	*Turn right*	*Go straight*
Go	*Try*	*Stop*
Stop	*Head east/west/north/south*	

Use your compass rose to help you write the correct direction words:
North, Northeast
East, Southeast
South, Southwest
West, Northwest

When writing your directions, please include:
- a *Start* and *End* place (dock, airport)
- at least 5 stops (places to visit) on your tour; e.g., ice cream shop, roller coaster, Lake _____, _____ Mountain, Magical Forest, market, waterfall
- direction words
- things to bring; e.g., map, money, backpack, sunscreen, towel, camera
- a compass rose
- 1 or 2 travel tips

WHAT: Taking A Tour of _____ Island

WHAT to Bring:

_____

_____

HOW to spend your day:

_____

_____

_____

_____

Tips:

_____

_____

© 2014 *Nonfiction Writing Power* by Adrienne Gear. Pembroke Publishers. ISBN 978-1-55138-293-7

How-to-Be-_____ Planning Page

Name: _____

Equipment	Physical Skills
_____	_____
_____	_____
_____	_____
_____	_____
_____	_____
_____	_____
_____	_____
_____	_____
_____	_____
_____	_____
_____	_____
_____	_____

Personality Traits	Tips from the Experts
_____	_____
_____	_____
_____	_____
_____	_____
_____	_____
_____	_____
_____	_____
_____	_____
_____	_____
_____	_____
_____	_____
_____	_____

Raccoon Samples

Sample 1: Racoons

A racoon is a nocturnal mammal that lives in wooded areas of North America. Raccoons have a long thick, grayish coat and a bushy tail with black rings. They have a band of black fur on their face that looks like a mask. Racoons live in the forest and like to be near water. They live in hollow trees, caves, or burrows. Their home is called a den. They sleep most of the day and come out at night to look for food. They can see very well at night and their eyes shine in the dark. Raccoons are omnivores—they eat plants, animals, and fish. They like to play with their food before they eat it. They are also very smart and often look for food in garbage cans. Enemies of the raccoon are coyotes, owls, bobcats, and foxes. Racoons are good climbers and swimmers. They will sometimes climb trees to get away from enemies.

Sample 2: How to Be a Racoon

Find your home in the forest near water.
Climb trees to escape from enemies and climb down head-first.
Sleep in the day and hunt at night.
Eat plants, meat, and fish.
Play with your food.
Use your bushy tail for balance.
Open garbage cans with your paws and look for food.
Beware of bobcats, foxes, and coyotes.
Be curious and clever.

© 2014 *Nonfiction Writing Power* by Adrienne Gear. Pembroke Publishers. ISBN 978-1-55138-293-7

How-to-Be-an-Animal Planner

Name: _____

Appearance	Habitat
_____	_____
_____	_____
_____	_____
_____	_____
_____	_____
_____	_____
_____	_____
_____	_____
Food	**Enemies**
_____	_____
_____	_____
_____	_____
_____	_____
_____	_____
_____	_____
_____	_____
_____	_____
Behavior	**Special Characteristics**
_____	_____
_____	_____
_____	_____
_____	_____
_____	_____
_____	_____

© 2014 *Nonfiction Writing Power* by Adrienne Gear. Pembroke Publishers. ISBN 978-1-55138-293-7

Handbook Planning Page

Name: _____

Equipment and Accessories	Personality Traits
Transportation	Food
Daily Activities	Home
Special Training	Beware of…
Fun Facts	Tips

6 The Power to Persuade

Children learn to persuade from a very early age. From before they can speak, some learn they can use their vocal chords or physical force to persuade their parents to give them another candy, let them stay longer at the park, or not put them into their car seat. From an early age, they are bombarded with persuasive advertising that convinces them that they must have the latest and greatest remote-control car or fashion-designer doll. As they get older and begin to form their own opinions and ideas, they learn to persuade others to read a certain book, go to a particular movie, or listen to a certain song on the radio. Children, in fact, have experienced the power of persuasion long before we teach it to them. Our job, as I see it, is to give this type of communication a name and provide them with the structure and language that will enhance what and how they communicate to share their opinions and learn to persuade others.

Again, one of the most important things a writer can do is connect to the reader. If done well, persuasive writing is the most powerful way we can make that connection. In persuasive writing, the writer's intent is often to directly persuade the reader to agree or disagree with a position or to take some kind of action. Mastering the power of persuasion will provide students with important tools for real-life experiences, such as writing a letter of complaint, participating in a debate, or applying for a job—all situations in which knowledge of persuasive writing is essential.

As with the other text structures, once students understand the basic form and language features, the creative possibilities are endless. I like to spend several weeks providing students with many opportunities to practice persuasive writing on a variety of different topics (see list on page 103). As with the other nonfiction forms of writing, once the structure of persuasive writing is understood by your students, it is exciting to link this writing form to your content areas.

Overview of Persuasive Writing

PERSUASIVE WRITING AT A GLANCE

Purpose
- To give an opinion or a point of view
- To justify a position
- To persuade or convince your reader
- To encourage reader to purchase something, participate in a specific activity, or think in a certain way

Text Structure: What–Why–Why–Why–What Was That Again?

1. **What your opinion is**
2. **Why:** Reason 1
3. **Why:** Reason 2
4. **Why:** Reason 3
5. **What Was That Again?:** restate your opinion

Language Features

- Usually in a knowledgeable and passionate voice
- Persuasive verbs: e.g., *should, need, must, I believe, I feel strongly*
- Persuasive adverbs: e.g., *definitely, absolutely, most certainly, without a doubt*
- Clear, strong reasons to support your position
- Examples and facts to back up your reasons
- Transition words: e.g., *first, next, finally*

Examples

- Newspaper advertisements
- Blogs
- Online gaming reviews
- Flyers
- Posters
- Book or movie reviews
- Letters
- Debates
- Speeches
- Advertisements
- Travel brochures
- Opinion pieces
- Editorials

Persuasive Anchor Books

Jamie Bastedo, *Free as the Wind: Saving the Horses on Sable Island* (P, I)

Mike Boldt, *1, 2, 3 versus A, B, C* (P, I)

Lauren Child, *I Wanna Pet* (P, I)

Doreen Cronin, *Click, Clack, Moo* (P)

Drew Daywalt, *The Day the Crayons Quit* (P, I)

Pamela W. Jane, *Should We Have Pets? A Persuasive Text* (P, I)

Martin Jenkins, *Can We Save the Tiger?* (P, I)

Steven Layne, *My Brother Dan's Delicious* (P, I)

Philip and Hannah Noose, *Hey, Little Ant!* (P, I)

Karen Orloff, *I Wanna Iguana* (P, I)

Karen Orloff, *I Wanna New Room* (P, I)

Lane Smith, *Glasses – Who Needs 'Em?* (P, I)

Tony Stead, *Should There Be Zoos?* (P, I)

Mark Teague, *Dear Mrs. LaRue* (I)

Judith Viorst, *Earrings!* (I)

Mélanie Watt, *Have I Got a Book for You!* (P, I)

P = primary
I = intermediate
Note that book level is a suggestion only; all books can be used at any level. See page 23. See also page 111 for how fiction books listed here can be used as models of persuasive writing.

Intent

The intent of persuasive writing varies, depending on topic and pupose, but all share the important purpose of stating a position and justifying it. Whether it be an opinion piece, in which the intent is simply to share an opinion, or a persuasive piece, for which the intent is to encourage some form of action from the reader (to purchase something, to attend an event or visit a specific place, to think in a certain way), the writer's intent is to share his or her opinion, belief, or stand on a particular issue and to back it up with clear reasons.

Form

Persuasive writing begins with a title and/or opening statement that clearly indicates the topic or subject being discussed or the position the writer is taking. The writer then provides a series of reasons or arguments to support that position. Persuasive texts end with a summary or conclusive statement that restates the opinion or position.

The rhyme pattern developed to help students remember the form of persuasive writing sounds like this: What–Why–Why–Why–What was that again?

1. *What* your opinion or position is
2. *Why*: reason 1
3. *Why*: reason 2
4. *Why*: reason 3
5. *What was that again?* Conclusion and restating of your opinion

Language Features

The following are language features commonly found in persuasive writing:

- Usually in a knowledgeable and passionate voice
- Persuasive verbs: e.g., *should, need, must, I believe, I feel strongly*
- Persuasive adverbs: e.g., *definitely, absolutely, most certainly, without a doubt*
- Connective phrases that have to do with reasoning: *because of, so, therefore*
- Transition words: e.g., *first, next, finally*

Writing Techniques

Because the connection to reader is crucial to persuasive writing, it is important for a writer to use a number of writing techniques that enhance voice and style. The following are writing techniques that can be introduced or reviewed as mini-lessons during your focus on persuasive writing:

- Voice (see lesson on pages 40 and 103)
- Triple-Scoop Words: using strong, sophisticated language is key to this form of writing (see lesson on page 38)
- Organization: the form of persuasive writing fits well with the "drawer" format (see lesson on page 43)

Links to Content Areas

When linking persuasive writing to content areas, the possibilities are endless. Students will need to research these topics beforehand in order to acquire the necessary background information to support their positions. Here are some suggestions of ways to link instructional writing to your social studies or science topics.

Science	Social Studies
Plants/Trees: plant catalogue **Animals/Insects/Dinosaurs**: the best pet; the animal that best symbolizes Canada; animal for a new coin; bird, animal, insect, fish—which would I rather be? **Space/ Planets**: _____ is the most interesting planet (or planet I'd like to live on); sun or moon—which is most important? **Natural Resources**: pipelines—helpful or harmful?; which natural resource is most important to us? **Human Body**: most important body system **Seasons**: _____ is the best season **Weather**: which extreme weather is most dangerous **Extreme Environment**: _____ is the most dangerous environment to live in **Health**: why exercise/ healthy eating/ is important	**Community**: the best school, best city, best community; best/most important occupation **Countries**: travel brochures (best country to visit) **Explorers**: the most important/ influential explorer **Ancient Civiliation**: the most influential invention of the past; clothing catalogue; civilization I would most liked to have lived in **Peoples**: most influential person in history **First Nations**: region I would most like to have lived in (Plains, Arctic, Woodlands); clothing catalogue **Government:** class/school election speeches **Celebrations around the World**: the best/most important cultural celebration, holiday **Famous Landmark or Structure**: the most amazing natural (or man-made) wonder of the world

Assessment

Here is an assessment rubric you can use when evaluating your students' persuasive writing pieces. These should be used to give your students feedback for their writing as well as provide you with a way of tracking trends in your class which may guide your instruction.

NY = Not Yet Meeting expectations
M = Meeting expectations (minimal level)
FM = Fully Meeting expectations
Ex = Exceeding expectations

PERSUASIVE WRITING ASSESSMENT RUBRIC

Title:	NY	M	FM	Ex
Form: Strong opening that clearly states an opinion or position.				
Organization: Five clear paragraphs that follow the persuasive text structure of What–Why–Why–Why–What was that again?				
Writing: Provides clear reasons and examples to back up opinion.				
Style: There is voice, evidence of persuasive language.				
Mechanics: Writing demonstrates effective use of spelling, punctuation, and grammar.				

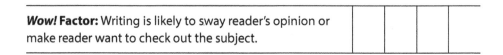

Wow! **Factor:** Writing is likely to sway reader's opinion or make reader want to check out the subject.			

Introduction to Persuasive Writing

Young children can be very opininated when it comes to their likes and dislikes. If you listen in on conversations at recess, it is not unusual to hear children debating over which is the best video game or the best song. Connecting persuasive writing to real-life experiences is a good way to introduce the structure of persuasive writing without requiring research.

- Write the following on the board or interactive whiteboard:

  What is the best TV show? The worst TV show?

- Ask students to think about how they would answer this. Ask them if they think everyone in the class will have the same opinion? (no) Why? (because different people like different things)
- Have students share their "best" and "worst" TV shows with a partner. Invite a few to share with the class. This can generate a lively discussion, as often children have very strong opinions! Remind students that when we are sharing opinions, there is no "right" or "wrong" and that we need to be respectful of others.
- Pass out the Bests and Worsts sheet (page 112) and allow time for students to fill in as many as they are able. Let them know that if they have blanks on their paper, it's okay. Invite students to share with a partner when they are finished.
- Explain to students that they have just given their opinion about several topics.

  What is important, when giving your opinion, is that you that you are able to justify, or back up, your reasons for having that opinion. It's sometimes easy to give our opinion about what we like or don't like, but harder to explain *why*.

Make sure names and dates are on these! I like to have the students write a *before* piece (i.e., before any instruction) so that I can compare a student's first piece of persuasive writing to their final piece.

- Pass out paper or have students take out their writer's notebooks. Tell them that you would like them to choose one of their *Best*s from the page and write about why they like it best.
- The next day, tell students that you have read their writing; tell them that some of their opinion pieces were a little confusing and not all of them were very convincing. Remind students that every form of writing has an inner skeleton or structure, and it's imporant for a writer to understand and follow the structure when writing.

  For the next few weeks, we are going to be practicing a form of writing called *persuasive* writing. The purpose of persuasive writing is to share an opinion or point of view with your reader. Sometimes, our intent is to share our opinion with our readers and explain why we think this way. Other times, our intent is to state our opinion and try to convince our readers to change their minds, to do something, or to buy something. This is called persusasive writing. But whether you are sharing your opinion or trying to persuade, you, as the writer, must clearly state your point of view and give good reasons why you think this way.

I sometimes use the analogy of building a house when teaching nonfiction writing. Builders start with the frame of a house first, then they add the details of the rooms. But if the frame is not solid, the house will fall down. Writers are like builders; i.e., they need to start with a solid frame or else their writing will fall apart!

- Explain that the structure or skeleton for persuasive writing sounds like this: What–Why–Why–Why–What Was That Again? Have them repeat this a few times with you while you list the words on the board.

  What your belief, opinion, postion, or point of view is
  Why: Reason 1 to support or back up your opinion
  Why: Reason 2 to support or back up your opinion
  Why: Reason 3 to support or back up your opinion
  What was that again?: Restate your belief, opinion, or point of view

Remind them that, as with all nonfiction writing forms, knowing the structure or skeleton is very important for the writer. Following this structure will help make our writing clear and easy to follow.

Features of Persuasive Writing

Before launching into persuasive writing lessons with your class, it is important to spend some time focusing on the key features of this form of writing: following the "sandwich plan" and using strong persuasive, transition, and descriptive words. Depending on your grade level, you might want to introduce these lessons over a few periods.

- Begin the lesson:

  Every form of writing has a few important key features that distinguish it from other forms of writing. We learned yesterday that the skeleton of persuasive writing follows the What–Why–Why–Why–What Was That Again? pattern. Today we are going to look at the important features.

FEATURE 1: THE SANDWICH PLAN

- Explain that one of the most important things a writer needs to do when writing a persuasive piece is to make a plan. Planning helps the writer organize his/her thinking before starting to write.
- Explain that they are going to learn the "sandwich plan" for persuasive writing.

The sandwich analogy can be useful when conferencing with students. After reading over their writing, I might say, "Oh, you have too much lettuce but no meat" or "You forgot your bottom slice of bread," and they know exactly what that means.

  Persuasive writing is a bit like making a sandwich. First, you have to start with the bread – the bread is *what*.
  (Draw a sideview of a piece of bread on the board.)
  Now I need to add some filling to my sandwich, so I think I will add some lettuce first.
  (Draw a sideview of a piece of lettuce on top of the bread; label it if you like.)
  This is my first *why*, or reason to back up my argument Now, I'm not sure about you, but I don't think I'd find a lettuce sandwich very tasty; in fact it would probably taste pretty boring. So I need to add another filling, like some cheese.
  (Add a layer of cheese to visual.)
  This is your second reason *why*. Cheese and lettuce taste better than just lettuce, but I really think I'd like some ham too.
  (Add ham to visual.)
  This is my third reason *why*. Now my sandwich is much tastier because I have three fillings instead of just one. But there is a slight problem. What's missing from my sandwich? (top slice of bread) If I don't have a top to my sandwich, it's going to fall apart. That's why I always need to add that second piece of bread.

(Add piece of bread to the visual.)

And this is when I restate or tell my reader again what my opinion is.

FEATURE 2: PERSUASIVE LANGUAGE

- Remind students that they are learning the features of persuasive writing. Tell them that, as well as following the structure, it is also important that they learn some key words used in this type of writing. These words will help their writing be more interesting and more organized. Refer to My Writing Goals chart (see page 34).
- Explain that there are three types of words used in persuasive writing: opinion words, transition words, and descriptive words.

I like to refer to transition words as "mayonnaise words," because they help your sandwich stick together!

The chart below can be used to introduce the various language features of persuasive writing. Students can copy these words onto the Persuasive Writing Language Features organizer (page 114) to keep as a reference in their writing folders or duotangs.

Persuasive Words	Transition Words	Descriptive Words
should	*First*	*amazing*
need	*Second, secondly*	*outstanding*
must	*Third, thirdly*	*unbelievable*
absolutely	*Next*	*adorable*
strongly believe	*Also*	*exciting*
definitely	*In addition*	*undeniable*
of course	*Another reason*	*marvelous*
it is my opinion	*Finally*	*beautiful*
absolutely		*delicious*
without a doubt		*fabulous*
I feel strongly		*fantastic*

- I often refer to descriptive words as the writer's chance to brag to the reader. Writers use bragging words when describing their subject in a convincing way. Explain that these words are often dependent on the topic you are writing about. Model a few examples:

  Place—*beautiful, spectacular, amazing, peaceful*
  Toy—*long-lasting, durable, safe*
  Food—*delicious, savory, mouth-watering*
  Book—*amazing, exciting, powerful, thoughtful*

LESSON SUMMARY: ANCHOR CHART

Review the goals for persuasive writing and create an anchor chart for future reference.

> **Persuasive Writing**
>
> - Includes a title
> - Clearly states the writer's opinion at the beginning
> - Follows the sandwich structure: What–Why–Why–Why–What Was That Again?
> - Gives clear reasons with examples
> - Includes strong persuasive words
> - Use transition (mayo) words: e.g., *first, next, also, finally*

Whole-Class Write

This whole-class write combines teacher modeling with independent writing. Students will be working independently on their own piece while you model and guide them with your own piece of writing.

- Create the following chart on the board or interactive whiteboard.

  _____ is the best season.

Fall	Winter
Spring	Summer

- Ask students to decide which season they think is the best. They might refer back to their Bests and Worsts sheets.
- Invite students to sign their names on the chart in the appropriate box; model by signing your own name.

Interactive Plan

- Remind students that all good writers make a plan. Explain that you are going make a sandwich plan for your piece about your favorite season. Use The Sandwich Plan for Persuasion template from page 113 for your model (see sample below):

  My favorite season is fall—that is my opinion, or my top slice of bread. Next, I have to think about my sandwich filling: three reasons why I like fall. I can think of lots of reasons, but I need to decide on three clear reasons.

- Invite students to help you think of reasons you might like this season. List one reason in each box.
- Explain that you need to include examples for each reason. Ask students to help you with this, and record their ideas as you continue to complete the plan.
- Restate your opinion at the bottom and explain that you need to summarize your ideas.

SAMPLE PLAN: MY FAVORITE SEASON

State your opinion: *My favorite season is fall*

Reason 1: *Colors—orange, red, gold (leaves) orange and black (Halloween), red poppy*

Reason 2: *Celebrations—Thanksgiving, Halloween, my birthday*

Reason 3: *Changes in weather—cool air, frost, first snow*

Restate your opinion: *My favorite season is fall – amazing colors, many celebrations, changes in weather*

- Remind students that this is just the plan. Explain that when they begin writing, they will need to "fill their drawers" (this can often lead to a few giggles!) by adding details and examples. Explain that each section of the planning page is one "drawer" (see Organization lesson on page 43).
- Refer back to the seasons chart and remind students that they have already decided on the season they prefer.
- Copy and hand out The Sandwich Plan for Persuasion and provide time for them to complete it.

Interactive Draft

- Once the students have completed their plan, it's important to review the language features with them and model how to "fill their drawers" with interesting and engaging sentences.

> Now that we have completed our plan, we are going to begin to develop our ideas into a piece of writing. Remember that a drawer has more than one or two socks in it, so we need to add several sentences to each section of our writing. We also need to be thinking of persuasive words connected to our topic.

You might wish to share the My Favorite Season model with the students on an overhead or interactive whiteboard, where you can highlight the key features as you read.

- Brainstorm words that can be connected to the topic of favorite season: *enjoyable, fun, delightful, exciting, beautiful, crisp, relaxing, quiet.*
- Discuss opening statements. Explain that writing "Fall is my favorite season and here are my reasons why" is not going to invite your reader to want to read on. (See Introductions to Hook Your Reader lesson on page 42.) Explain that describing a scene using the senses or asking a question would be a better way to start. Share the first paragraph of the model text My Favorite Season (page 115). Ask students what they noticed.
- Invite students to write their first paragraph only. Encourage them to try to use some of the techniques to state their opinion, but to do it in a way that their reader will be hooked, or interested.

- Model the second "drawer" and ask students what they noticed. Highlight key words and features that are important for persuasive writing.
- Students can begin to rewrite their own favorite-season piece, trying to include the features of persuasive writing they have learned. Review the anchor chart on page 101.
- Once they have finished their drafts, students can read and conference with a partner and then spend some time editing and revising (see editing checklists on page 25).

Independent Write

The Weekly Topic

The more opportunities students are given to practice writing their opinion on a topic using the structure and langauge of persuasion, the more confident and competent they will become. I recommend starting with topics that do not require additional research and that are relevant to your students lives:

Should We Have Zoos? by Tony Stead and *Should We Have Pets?* by Pamela Jane are excellent persuasive anchor books and provide examples of persuasive arguments written by students.

- Should there be zoos?
- Should we wear school uniforms?
- Should cell phones be allowed in school?
- Should we have homework?
- Should electronic screentime be limited for kids?
- Should gum be allowed in school?
- Should we have pets?
- Should bears be killed if they come into yards?

I usually base my writing schedule for these practice pieces on the writing process, spread out over three to four days:

- Plan: Write the statement at the top of a T-chart on the board or chart paper and invite students to agree or disagree by writing their name in the Yes or No column that reflects their opinion. They can then use the sandwich plan on page 113 to complete their plan.
- Draft: Students can begin writing their pieces, using their planning sheet and filling the "drawers" with clear examples.
- Conference/Edit: Once they have finished their drafts, students can read and conference with a partner and then spend some time editing and revising (see editing checklists on page 25).

Providing regular assessment and feedback to students will promote improved writing skills. The Persuasive Writing Assessment Rubric on page 97 can be used to provide regular feedback to the students for their weekly writing.

Voice in Persuasive Writing

- Begin the lesson:

Anchor Book: *The Perfect Puppy for Me!* by Jane O'Connor provides facts and opinions about different breeds of dogs, and would be a good model for this lesson.

We have been practicing persuasive writing. We have learned the structure of this kind of writing and some of the important words that can help make your persuasive writing more organized and clearer. Today we are going to learn something that can help make your writing more interesting to read, which is one of our Writing Goals. (Refer to the My Writing Goals chart; see page 34.)

- Give a copy of Cats Are the Best Pet (page 116) to each student. Ask them to read the text samples or read them aloud yourself. Ask them to pay attention to what makes the writing in the two samples different and which one is more interesting to read.
- After reading both samples, ask students to discuss what is different. Both writers appear to be following the correct structure, but which one is more interesting to read? (the second one) Why? (because it has voice)
- Explain that *voice* is something writers use when they want to make their writing more interesting and more engaging. When you write only facts, sometimes it becomes a little boring to read. Voice helps keep the reader interested.
- Tell students they are going to be writing a piece about pets. They will be choosing the best pet and trying to use voice in their writing.
- Brainstorm a list of possible pets on the board. (dogs, cats, fish, hamsters, snakes, budgies) Brainstorm possible reasons why a pet might be the best. (cute, smart, easy to care for, easy to train, loyal, helpful)
- Ask students to think about which pet they think is the best and why. They need three reasons with examples. Have students share and compare with a partner.
- Since some students work better with list plans and some work better with web plans (see page 56), students can choose The Best Pet Planner 1 on page 117 or The Best Pet Planner 2 on page 118 to complete.
- Remind students of the goals for this form of writing by looking at the anchor chart (page 101). Add *Voice* to the anchor chart and tell students you will be looking for voice in their pieces.

Using Facts in Persuasive Writing

Using what they have learned about opinion writing, students choose a topic they are interested in and have some knowledge about.

- Write the following phrase on the chart stand or board:

_____ is the best _____

- Explain that students will be choosing their own topic and writing their opinion about it. Ask them how they would complete the sentence on the board.
- Brainstorm some possibilities: *basketball is best sport; Henrik Sedin is the best hockey player; Taylor Swift is the best singer.* Other ideas might be to identify the best group, best teacher, best smart phone, best book, best movie, best TV show, best war hero, best city, best friend, best brother, etc.
- Remind students that they need to be able to think of three clear reasons why they like the subject of their writing; they need to give examples to support the reasons.
- Give students time to think about, choose, and share their writing topic with a partner.
- Students can choose to use the Persuasive List Planner (page 119), the Persuasive Web Planner (page 120), or the sandwich planner (page 113) for their planning.
- Model how to complete the planner, focusing on examples for each reason. Invite students to add ideas while you complete the plan.

Opinion: Sexsmith School is the Best School EVER! Details: location, number of students, principal

Reason 1: Great teachers. Examples: make learning fun, field trips, care about kids

Reason 2: Lots of great activities. Examples: Green Team, Student Council, sports teams

Reason 3: Great kids. Examples: polite, smart, helpful

- Explain that when someone is writing an opinion, real facts can help support the opinion and make it stronger. Ask students which is more convincing: "She has lots of hit records" or "She has had five number-one hits in the past three years."
- Encourage students to include at least one true fact to support each opinion, if possible. Ask students what real fact to include in your plan to help support your opinion. (sports records or scores, age of school)
- Provide time for students to complete filling out their planning pages.
- Students can use their plans to begin their writing. Use the anchor chart and remind them that you will be looking for supporting facts in their writing.

Opinion vs Persuasion

How does persuasive writing differ from opinion writing? Here is the simplified answer to the question: the difference is *action*. In an opinion piece, I am giving my opinion but I am not trying to promote any action in my reader. In fact, I may not really care what my reader thinks; my intent is to share my opinion and explain why I think that. With persuasive writing, I am still giving my opinion about something; however, I am now eliciting some form of action from my reader.

Anchor Books

Lauren Child, *I Want a Pet* (P, I)

Lois G. Grambling, *Can I Bring My Pterodactyl to School, Ms. Johnson?* (P)

Lois G. Grambling, *Can I Have a Tyrannosaurus, Mom? Can I? Please?* (P)

Steven Kellogg, *Can I Keep Him?* (P)

Karen Orloff, *I Wanna Iguana* (P, I)

Karen Orloff, *I Wanna New Room* (P, I)

Margie Palatini, *The Perfect Pet* (P)

Judith Viorst, *Earrings!* (I)

P = primary
I = intermediate
Note that book level is a suggestion only; all books can be used at any level. See page 23.

In this lesson, students will learn the difference between opinion and persuasion; they will use their new understanding to write a persuasive letter to their parents.

- Begin the lesson:

  We've been learning how to form an opinion and write reasons to support that opinion. Today we are going to look at a different way we can write our opinion. It's called *persuasion*. It follows the same structure as opinion writing: What–Why–Why–Why–What Was That Again? But this time there is a difference. I have a few books I want to share that model this type of persuasive writing.

- Read *I Wanna Iguana* or any of the anchor books listed. Use the following questions for class discussion:

  - What kind of writing is this showing?

- What is the character trying to do? (convince his mom to let him keep the iguana)
- How does he get his mom to change her mind? (gives many convincing reasons)
- How is this different from the writing we did about the best pet? (best pet was just giving our opinion)

- Explain that sometimes writers want to share their opinion about something, but other times they want to share their opinion and also try to convince or persuade the reader to agree with them.
- Write the words *Opinion* and *Persuasion* on the board or interactive whiteboard. Give students the example topic "Dogs are the Best Pet" and ask them what the difference would be between an opinion and a persuasion. (Opinion: writer telling readers why they think dogs are the best pet; Persuasion: writer telling readers that dogs are the best pet and that they should have one)
- Go through this exercise (opinion vs. persuasion) with other topics: books, toys, video games, movies, foods, sport. Remind students that persuasion requires some form of action from the reader. Here are a couple of examples for students to use to distinguish between opinion and persuasion:

    Stanley Park is one of my favorite places in Vancouver. There is a lot to do there. (Opinion)
    I definitely think you should visit Stanley Park because there is so much to do there. (Persuasion)

    My favorite drink is 7-Up. I like the clear, sweet, bubbly taste, and the lemon and lime flavors are more refreshing than other pop. (Opinion)
    7-Up is the best drink ever! This refreshing, sweet, bubbly drink is better than any other drink. You should definitely drink 7-Up next time you are thirsty! (Persuasion)

- Older students can practice by developing their own opinion statement and persuasive statement about the same topic.
- Invite students to think about something they really wanted and tried to persuade their parents to let them do or have. Brainstorm ideas: to have their own room; to get an allowance or increase in allowance; to take lessons in something; to not take lessons in something; to have a sleepover; to go to a movie; to stay up later; to have a pet; to have a computer or a cell phone; to go on a trip; to buy a toy, video game, or item of clothing.
- Explain that they are going to write a letter to their parents, trying to persuade them to take action somehow. (Students can choose whether or not to actually give their letters to their parents.) Tell them that if they write a very persuasive letter with good reasons, perhaps they will get what they want!
- Pass out planning sheets. Students may choose from the the Persuasive List Planner (page 119), the Persuasive Web Planner (page 120), and the Sandwich Plan for Persuasion (page 113). Invite students to begin planning their persuasive letters. Remind them that the success of the letter will depend on how well they present their case!
- Tell students that they will still be using the sandwich structure (page 99), but that they need to write it in the form of a letter. Review the key features of a letter they will need to include: date, greeting, closing, signature.

After doing this lesson several times with different classes, I find that many students try to convince their parents through bribes: e.g., "If you get me an iPad, I promise that I will keep my room clean." I suggest that you discuss the difference between *a bribe* and *a reason* before they begin. I tell them that they may "sweeten the pot" in their letter with one perk, but that the persuasion also needs to include legitimate reasons.

Writing a Book Review

Writing a book talk or book review is a great opportunity for students to practice persuasive writing. In the past, when I asked my students to prepare a book talk, I have been disappointed with the lack of substance in their writing. "I liked this book. It was good" was often as far as some were able to go. In reflecting on this, I realize the lack of conviction in their writing was due, in part, to my failure to provide explicit instruction in persuasive writing.

If possible, bring one of your favorite books into class and model your own book talk!

- Ask students, "What's the best book you have ever read?" Brainstorm a list of titles. Ask, "What makes a book good?" Brainstorm possibilities: exciting plot, funny, great characters, suspenseful, interesting, etc.
- Explain that they will be writing a persuasive book review: they will write about their favorite book, trying to persuade others to read it too. The book reviews will be presented to the class.
- Ask students what they think would be important to include in their writing. Create an anchor chart:

Have I Got a Book for You! by Mélanie Watt is a hilarious book about a book review, and is an excellent model of how to include voice in persuasive writing.

> A Good Book Review includes
> - Attention-grabbing opening
> - Title and author at the beginning and the end
> - Genre: e.g., fiction, nonfiction, adventure, series, humor
> - General summary of what the book is about: make it short and to the point – but no spoilers!
> - Description of favorite part or favorite character
> - A possible connection to another book or your own life
> - Who might want to read this book: e.g., "If you really like adventure books…"

Students can continue practicing review writing by writing about their favorite movie or video game.

- As always, students will need time to plan their piece of writing and to make sure they have three clear reasons why they like the book. Students should prepare to read their review to the class.
- Remind students that part of your evaluation will be on their presentation and how well they are able to "sell" their book to the class. While I don't insist on memorizing, it is important to explain and model the difference between someone talking about the book and someone simply reading about the book.

Persuasive Writing to Influence Change

Anchor Books

Laurie Hall Anderson, *Thank You, Sarah: The Woman Who Saved Thanksgiving* (P, I)
Jamie Bastedo, *Free as the Wind: Saving the Horses on Sable Island* (P, I)

Ruth Brown, *The World that Jack Built* (P, I)
Gail Gibbons, *Recycle: A Handbook for Kids* (P, I)

P = primary
I = intermediate
Note that book level is a suggestion only; all books can be used at any level. See page 23.

Writing is powerful and, if done well, can influence people to create change. When you feel very strongly about something, writing is a way to express yourself and to possibly effect change. In this lesson, students will have an opportunity to develop a piece of writing that is intended to influence change.

• Begin the lesson:

> Sometimes people write in order to make changes in the world. In the news you might see people protesting about something. Maybe trees are going to be cut down to build a mall and the people in the neighborhood are protesting. Maybe a hospital is going to be shut down and people protest against that. Maybe an oil pipeline is going to affect the animals in a wilderness area. When people feel very strongly about something, they often write a persuasive letter to try to express their belief and to influence change.

• Read *Free as the Wind* by Jamie Bastedo. This book is the true story of school children who wrote letters to try to save the horses on Sable Island, Nova Scotia, from being killed. It is an excellent example of persuasive writing being used to influence change. Discuss how writing these letters resulted in change that helped save the lives of the wild horses.

• Brainstorm different issues that are relevant to students:

> Personal issues: e.g., getting a pet, a cell phone, a new computer, your own room
> School issues: e.g., longer recess; wearing uniforms; competitive sports day; afternoon recess; junkfood in schools
> Community issues: e.g., don't close the hospital, don't build another mall; we need a new playground; public transportation, bike lanes; grow and eat locally; child poverty; recycling
> National issues: e.g., gun laws; animals in captivity; healthcare; drugs
> Global issues: e.g., war; caring for the environment; child poverty; child slavery

• Students choose one issue they feel is important to them. Check the local newspaper for current events in your city that could provide relevant topics for these letters. As in previous lessons, students should be given time to plan their letters using the sandwich plan (see page 113).

• Review the features of persuasive writing and remind students that, when writing to influence change, their writing must use a respectful tone. Remind students that the intent of the letter is to promote or influence change in some way, and that they must be very clear in stating their opinion and what they hope will happen. Depending on the topic of the letter, students should address the letter to a specific person; e.g., their parents, the principal, the mayor, a member of parliament, etc.

Persuasive Writing Extensions

New Five-Dollar Coin

Explain to students that the government is considering stopping production of the five-dollar bill and replacing it with a new coin. Make connections to other large-denomination coins; e.g., the loonie and toonie; the Sacajawea dollar. Students are to decide which person, animal, or item would be the best choice for the new coin. Brainstorm some ideas and discuss reasons why they would be good choices. This lesson does require some research, so would be a great way to tie in science or social studies. Students make their choices about the coin design,

This sample includes a persuasive letter, and is by a student in Grade 6.

including the following: metal used, image, dollar amount, date, country, border around the edge of the coin.

New $5.00 Coin!

Dear Minister of Finance,   Mar, 5/3013

Hi! My name is   and I am eleven years old. I'm in grade six and I go to J.W. Sexsmith Elementary School. I live in Vancouver, British Columbia, Canada. I am writing this letter to you because I have a symbol for the new $5 coin. It is Skates! Here are my reasons why!

The first reason why I want to put skates on the $5 coin is because of hockey. You probably know who Wayne Gretzky is and so he is probably the best player of all time! So when he won Stanley Cups and gold medals, he was representing Canada. Also in 2010 finals for hockey Canada won because of the Golden Goal scored by Sidney Crosby. That is something people will remember. Another reason is hockey is first originated in Canada so it is our main sport. That is my first reason why I think skates should be on the five dollar coin.

Secondly, why I think skates should be on the five dollar coin is that it will represent figure skating. The reason is when you are watching TV, and you go to the channel were figure skating is on you just flip the channel. Well people think

it's boring when they do the twirls. Actually it isn't it is amazing and fascinating when you see those twirls in the air and they land perfectly. Also those athletes who do that are professional and they spend lots of time doing their routine, and we don't appreciate that. That's not fair at all. My last reason is that Canada has some amazing figure skaters and they win lots of awards.   Who, name some famous Canadian skaters.

My last and final reason why skates should be on the five dollar coin is that it is a great symbol to represent Canada. It is great because, Canada is an outdoor cold country. It isn't a super-hot dessert. So that's why skates are a good symbol. Also it represents Canadian sports with skates for example like speed skating, figure skating and hockey. My last reason is that skating is an outside and inside sport because you can skate outside on the outdoor rink and, skate in an arena.

That's why I think skates should be on the five dollar coin. Also all Canadians love skating! It is a tradition!! I hope you enjoyed this letter! I wish I persuaded you!!!

Sincerely,

Persuasive Catalogues

Advertisements are excellent examples of persuasive texts, as they are written with the intent of persuading the reader to purchase something. Bring catalogues into class and discuss writer's intent and how this is a form of persuasive writing. Have students create catalogues for a science or social studies unit you are working on: e.g., a plant catalogue for study of plants; a clothing catalogue linked to a study of First Nations or ancient civilizations. Students would likely need to research special features of the products and how they are made.

This sample is by a student in Grade 4.

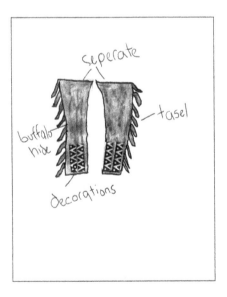

seperate

tasel

buffalo hide

decorations

Cree Leggings

Are you ready for the new generation of pants? Well, if you are, then this is the item for you! Cree Leggings are stylish and practical. The soft hide of the buffalo will provide you with ventilation, protection from rain and easy movement for hunting or shopping! They are worn under your breechcloth and wrap around your legs. In case you didn't know, these leggings come in a pair and you pull them up on each leg like a sock. They can either come plain, with side tassels or with tassels and decorations. Take your pick but hurry because they won't last long!

The Great Chocolate Challenge

Students work in groups of five to write a persuasive piece about chocolate bars. Each group is given one chocolate bar; their goal is to persuade the rest of the class that their chocolate bar is the best. Each group member is responsible for writing and presenting one of the five paragraphs:

- Opening
- Reason 1
- Reason 2
- Reason 3
- Closing

I usually give students one day to write and one day to practice; they present on day three. The winning team is the team that presents the most convicing argument about their chocoloate bar, as well as presents most effectively. Each member of the winning group receives a chocolate bar.

Class or School Elections

Anchor Book: Doreen Cronin, *Duck for President!*

Student elections are an excellent opportunity for students to apply their knowledge of persuasive writing to a real-life experience. Often, student candidates are asked to prepare a speech with the intent to convince their peers that they would make the best school president (or vice president, secretary, special events coordinator, etc.). Students can use their knowledge of the structure and language of persuasive writing to prepare a speech. Even students who are not officially running could be encouraged to write a speech.

Nursery Rhyme Letters

This persuasive writing piece combines knowledge of nursery rhymes with persuasive writing. Students select from a list of nursery rhymes or brainstorm a list in class. In character, students write a letter explaining their concerns to another character, for example:

- Mary writes a letter to the lamb to persuade him to stop following her.
- Little Miss Muffet writes to the spider to ask him to not scare her every morning.
- Peter Peter's wife writes to Peter to tell him to take her out of the pumpkin shell.
- Humpty Dumpty writes to the soldiers to beg to be put back together.
- Townspeople write to Wee Willie Winkie to ask him to not keep running around in his nightshirt.

Students can exchange letters with each other and write a response letter in character.

This sample is by a student in Grade 7.

> Dear Mr. Spider,
>
> Every morning when I am eating my curds and whey, under the oak tree. You, Mr. Spider, come down and frighten me. Do you know how many fright attacks I have had from you? No you don't so leave me alone. Don't you have a life? You are one mean, ugly looking spider. Now, I am going to say this as nicely as possible. "LEAVE ME ALONE!" What do you want from me? I am tired of making a new batch of curds and whey every morning. You are one skinny wimp. I have a life too, but no you just come down on your web and ruin everything. Please leave me alone!
>
> Sincerely,
> Scared LIttle Miss Muffet

Persuasive Writing from Different Points of View

There are many books in which the author uses persuasive writing from the point of view of various objects and animals. While these books are considered fiction with the intent to entertain, they are excellent examples of purposeful persuasive writing, and they can add humor and creativity to your weekly writing pieces.

- Drew Daywalt, *The Day the Crayons Quit*
  This book is written from the point of view of several crayons that "quit" because they are tired of how they are being used. Students can write a letter from the point of view of a crayon color, explaining why they are not happy with their situation.
- Doreen Cronin, *Click, Clack, Moo: Cows that Type*
  Cows, unhappy with their life, type letters to the farmer, demanding changes be made to their working conditions. Students could write letters from the point of view of a farm animal or pet, asking the owner for a variety of different things: better food, warmer bed, more outdoor time, etc.
- Mike Boldt, *1, 2, 3 vs A, B, C*
  Which are more important, letters or numbers? In this persuasive showdown, letters and numbers try to convince each other that they are the most important. Students could choose which they think is more important and write a persuasive piece about why. Each side could present their opinion in a class debate.
- Philip and Hannah Noose, *Hey, Little Ant*
  Hey, Little Ant presents two different points of view on squishing an ant: the ant's (who is about to be squished) and the boy's (who is about to do the squishing). The writer does an excellent job of using supportive reasons for both sides of the argument. After reading this anchor book, students could write a letter from an insect's perspective, presenting their argument why they should not be squished. Teachers could link this persuasive writing lesson to a science unit on insects and include research on facts about how the insect helps the environment in their argument.
- Steven L. Layne, *My Brother Dan's Delicious*
  In this humorous book, a boy tries to convince the monster in his closet to eat his brother, Dan, instead of him. After listening to this story, students could write their own *Dear Monster* letters.
- Marc Teague, *Dear Mrs. LaRue*
  Mrs. LaRue has just sent her dog Ike to obedience school. Ike is not happy with conditions at the school and is writing letters to his owner to persuade her to bring him back home. Students could write a persuasive letter from either an animal in a zoo or an animal in an obedience school, asking to be set free.

Bests and Worsts

Name: _____

What's Your Opinion?

Subject	Best	Worst
color		
season		
book		
TV show		
movie		
video game		
singer/singing group		
fictional character		
app		
smart phone		
video game console		
animal		
sport		
dessert		
flavor of ice cream		
drink		
dinner		
subject in school		
special day/celebration		
store		
candy		
vegetable		
place to travel/visit		
invention		

The Sandwich Plan for Persuasion

Name: _____

State your opinion:

_____

_____

_____

_____

Reason 1:

_____

_____

_____

_____

Reason 2:

_____

_____

_____

_____

Reason 3:

_____

_____

_____

_____

Restate your opinion:

_____

_____

_____

_____

Persuasive Writing Language Features

Name: _____

Opinion Words	Transition Words

Descriptive Words
Place:
Food:
Book:
Person:
Season:

My Favorite Season

The smell of frost in the air, the crunch of leaves, the beautiful colors of the trees—these are just some of the reasons I believe fall is definitely the best season! I look forward to fall every year and here's why.

First, the colors of fall are amazing! There are bright orange pumpkins in grocery stores and growing in fields. It is also fascinating to watch the colors of the leaves change from green to orange, red, yellow, and brown. On a sunny day the sky shines bright blue, and at night the mountains glow like pointy purple lanterns. Fall is definitely the most colorful season!

Another great thing about fall is the many activities and special celebrations that happen. There is Thanksgiving, when you eat delicious turkey with your family. And let's not forget the fun of Halloween! Remembrance Day is an important day in November to remember all the soldiers who fought in wars. There are also leaves to jump in and lots of activities you can do outside. Isn't fall fun?

Finally, I love the changes that happen in nature during the fall. The weather starts to change from hot to cool and the frost starts to appear in the mornings. I love the feel of the strong winds that blow the leaves all around. We change the clocks back as the days get shorter, and that always makes me want to curl up by the fire and read a book! Sometimes, snow starts to fall in the mountains so you can see the white snowcaps. This always makes me feel excited about a snowfall!

Well, there you have it! Fall is definitely my favorite season because of all the beautiful colors, the exciting activities, and the changes I can see in nature. It really is the very best season and I look forward to fall every year. What's your favorite season?

Cats Are the Best Pet

Sample 1

Cats are the best pet by far. They are small, cute, and furry and are easy to own. They purr and like to sleep on your bed and keep you company all day long. Let me tell you why I love cats.

First, cats are definitely easy to care for. They don't eat much and they don't need very much care. You don't have to walk them or give them a bath because they clean themselves. They don't really need a lot of attention because they sleep a lot so you don't have to worry about entertaining them.

Second, cats are smart. They can do tricks and also you can teach them to go to the bathroom outside or in the litter box. They also can find your house even if they go far away. Another thing is that they are smart enough to catch mice and rats.

Sample 2

You are sitting reading a book and relaxing. Suddenly, you feel this soft ball of fur around your feet and hear a soft purr. You look down and there it is, a fluffy, adorable little ball of fur called—you guessed it—a cat, the greatest, most amazing, bestest pet in the entire world. And if you don't believe me—just wait!

First of all, cats are super easy to care for. Cats are independent, and that means easy-peasy-lemon-squeezy cat care! No messy cage to clean, no poop to scoop, no baths to give. No, sir! They clean themselves, dig their own poop-hole in the garden—and cover it up—and you never have to give them a bath. Best of all, you don't have to take them for walks every day on a leash. They can stroll around the neighborhood, chilling with their feline friends, and they'll always come back to you. Just call their name or shake their box of cat food and they'll come a-running!

Another reason why cats are the best of all living creatures is that they are smart. You don't believe me? Well, how many times has a cat rescued you and your family from being invaded by mice? Have you ever tried to catch a mouse? Let's face it—it's not exactly easy-peasy-lemon-squeezy! Also, you can pretty much count on a cat to know where to use the facilities—that's toilet, for those of you who didn't know! They either go outside in the dirt (not in the grass like dogs) or in the litter box inside. That's definitely smart, if you ask me!

© 2014 *Nonfiction Writing Power* by Adrienne Gear. Pembroke Publishers. ISBN 978-1-55138-293-7

The Best Pet Planner 1

Name: _____

_____ Are The Best Pet Ever!

Opening:

_____
_____
_____

Reason 1:

_____
_____
_____

Reason 2:

_____
_____
_____

Reason 3:

_____
_____
_____

Closing:

_____
_____

The Best Pet Planner 2

Name: _____

Why is your pet the best pet ever?

Consider the following:

Appearance: Is your pet cute? cuddly? fluffy? small? big?

Size: Is your pet a good size? What makes it a good size?

Intelligence: Is your pet smart? easy to train?

Companionship: Is your pet friendly? a good house pet? good with children? protective?

Think about **descriptive words** to describe your pet:

adorable	friendly
cuddly	cooperative
soft	easy to care for
smart	magnificent
intelligent	protective
athletic	independent
cute	loyal

Persuasive List Planner

What? Your opinion or position	_____ _____ _____ _____ _____ _____
Why? Reason 1	_____ _____ _____ _____ _____ _____
Why? Reason 2	_____ _____ _____ _____ _____ _____
Why? Reason 3	_____ _____ _____ _____ _____ _____
What was that again? Restate your opinion.	_____ _____ _____ _____ _____

Persuasive Web Planner

Name: _____

_____

```
                    ↑
        ┌─────────────────────┐
        │      Reason 1       │
 ←──────┤                     ├──────→
        │  _____  │
        │  _____  │
        └─────────────────────┘
                    │
        ┌─────────────────────┐
        │  _____  │
        │  _____  │
        │  _____  │
        │  _____  │
        │  _____  │
        └─────────────────────┘
```

```
   ↑                                      ↑
┌─────────────────┐        ┌─────────────────┐
│    Reason 2     │        │    Reason 3     │
│                 │        │                 │
│  _____  │        │  _____  │
│  _____  │        │  _____  │
└─────────────────┘        └─────────────────┘
   │         │                │         │
   ↓         ↓                ↓         ↓
```

_____ _____   _____ _____

7 The Power to Compare

As students move into higher grades, they are expected to be able to write in a wide variety of different forms. No longer is the five-paragraph essay adequate to get a student through State or Provincial exams. Students are being asked to write in more complex forms, including comparisons. Introducing this form and the language associated with it to younger students can be the first steps in ensuring their success down the road.

Overview of Comparison Writing

COMPARISON WRITING AT A GLANCE

Purpose
- To describe similarities and differences between two or more topics
- To give a general description of each topic, focusing on specific features that make them similar or different

Text Structure: Both–Same–Different–Different–End
1. **Both:** Introduce things you are comparing
2. **Same:** How the two things are the same
3. **Different:** How the two things are different
4. **Different:** More differences (if needed)
5. **End:** Concluding statement

Language Features
- Use of factual descriptions
- Language of comparison: *but, in contrast, however, on the other hand, whereas, unlike, similarly, different, share, difference, compared to, while, although, as well as, not only, but also*
- Inclusion of Venn diagram, web, or matrix (chart) to illustrate comparisons

Examples
- Comparing two animals or insects: e.g., bee and wasp
- Comparing two habitats: e.g., forest and desert
- Comparing two sports: e.g., football and soccer
- Comparing two people: e.g., me and my friend
- Comparing two varieties of the same objects: e.g., iPhone and Samsung Galaxy; deciduous and evergreen trees; Toyota and Honda cars
- Comparing two countries: e.g., Spain and France
- Comparing two civilizations: e.g., Ancient Rome and Ancient Egypt
- Comparing two time periods: e.g., past and present
- Comparing two communities: e.g., urban and rural
- Comparing two homes: e.g., brick house and igloo

Comparison Anchor Books

Julie Cummins, *Country Kid, City Kid* (P, I)
Judy Diehl and David Plumb, *What's the Difference? 10 Animal Look-Alikes* (I)
Bobbie Katz, *We're Different; We're the Same* (P)
Jenny Sue Kostecki-Shaw, *Same, Same but Different* (P)
Debbie S. Miller, *Are Trees Alive?* (P, I)
Lisa Westberg Peters, *The Sun, the Wind and the Rain* (P, I)

Isabel Thomas, *Lions Vs. Tigers: Animals Head to Head* (I)
Isabel Thomas, *Shark Vs. Killer Whale: Animals Head to Head* (I)
Isabel Thomas, *Alligator Vs. Crocodile: Animals Head to Head* (I)

P = primary
I = intermediate
Note that book level is a suggestion only; all books can be used at any level. See page 23.

Intent

The intent of comparative writing is compare two or more subjects for the reader by outlining how the subjects are similar and how they differ. Depending on the topics being discussed, a writer can also include an opinion about one or the other topic as being the best, most dangerous, most interesting, most effective, most influential, etc.

Form

Comparative writing is usually divided into four distinct parts:

1. It begins with a clear introduction to the two (or more) subjects being discussed.
2. This is followed by a paragraph describing how the two subjects are similar.
3. The next paragraph outlines how the two subjects differ.
4. Finally, the writer summarizes the similarities and differences, and provides a concluding statement. Depending on the topic and intent, this conclusion might include the writer's opinion.

If there are more similarities or more differences, these middle sections might vary in length.

The rhyme pattern developed to help students remember the form of comparison sounds like this: Both–Same–Different–End

1. *Both*: the two (or more) subjects being compared
2. *Same*: how they are the same
3. *Different*: how they are different
4. *End*: summary and conclusion

Language Features

The following are features commonly found in comparison writing:

- Use of factual descriptions
- Language of comparison: *but, in contrast, however, on the other hand, whereas, unlike, similarly, different, share, difference, compared to, while, although, as well as, not only, but also,* etc.
- Inclusion of Venn diagram, web, or matrix (chart) to illustrate comparisons

Writing Techniques

Incorporating a variety of writing techniques into a comparative piece can help strengthen and enhance the writing style, and create a more engaging piece for the reader. The following are mini-lessons that could be introduced or reviewed during your focus on this form:

- Nonfiction Text Features: Venn diagram (see lesson on page 36)
- Voice (see lesson on page 40)
- Introductions to Hook Your Reader (see lesson on page 42)
- Interesting Details (see lesson on page 37)
- Organization (see lesson on page 43)

Links to the Content Areas

Linking comparison writing to your content areas provides students with an opportunity to practice the form, language, and intent with a wide range of topics. While comparing animals tends to be a good starting point for teaching comparative writing that incorporates research, there are many other topics in science and social studies that lend themselves to writing comparisons:

Science	Social Studies
• evergreen and deciduous trees • two plants: e.g., cactus and rose • two seasons: e.g., winter and summer • ponds and lakes • two habitats: e.g., desert and rainforest • seashore and garden • two planets: e.g., Jupiter and Mars	• two countries: e.g., Canada and Japan • two aboriginal groups: e.g., Cree and Haida • a child's life in Canada and in a developing country • past and present: homes, schools, clothes, education • transportation then and now • ancient civilizations • two government positions: e.g., President and Prime Minister • two occupations: e.g., doctor and nurse

Assessment

This rubric can be used as a benchmark for assessing your students' comparison writing pieces. As always, I encourage you to make adjustments to any of the comments to meet the needs of your specfic grade.

COMPARISON WRITING ASSESSMENT RUBRIC

NY = Not Yet Meeting expectations
M = Meeting expectations (minimal level)
FM = Fully Meeting expectations
Ex = Exceeding expectations

Title:	NY	M	FM	Ex
Form: Demonstrates the Both–Same–Different–End structure; uses specific examples to illustrate comparisons.				
Word Choice: Integrates the language of comparison appropriately.				
Organization: Compares and contrasts clearly; transitions smoothly from one idea to the next.				

Style: Engages the reader with interesting sentences and voice.			
Mechanics: Writing demonstrates effective use of spelling, punctuation, and grammar.			

Introduction to Comparison Writing

- Place an apple and an orange on the table. Ask students what the objects are. (apple, orange, fruit)
- Ask students how the objects are the same. (both fruit, grow on trees, round, good for you, can be made into juice)
- Ask students how the objects are different. (color, taste, texture)
- Introduce the concept of comparing:

    Sometimes, a writer chooses to write about one topic. We call this descriptive writing. But other times, a writer might want to compare two topics and describe how they are the same and how they are different. This type of writing is called *comparison*, because the writer is comparing two or more things.

- Explain that writers can compare two objects, two people, or two ideas. Brainstorm ideas for comparisons: cats and dogs, apples and oranges, iPhone 5 and iPhone 5S, Xbox and PS3, Harry Potter and Voldemort.
- Remind students that every text form has an inner skeleton or structure, and it's important for a writer to understand and follow the structure when writing.

    One of the challenges in comparisons is trying to write about two things at once. Switching back and forth between similarities and differences can be very confusing for you and your reader. Here is the skeleton of comparison writing that can help you to not get mixed up: Both–Same–Different–End. We start by introducing both topics; we write about how they are the same; then we write about how they are different; we add more differences if we need to; and then we write our ending. Following this structure can help our writing be organized and help our reader to not get confused.

- Model this structure by comparing the apple and orange. Invite students to help you.

For beginning writers, I use the simple framework of Both–Same–Different–End. Older students might need to include an additional paragraph of differences.

Both	Apple and orange
Same	fruit; grow on trees; can be made into juice; healthy; have seeds; can be sweet or sour
Different	Apples: hard; different colors and varieties; have a stem; inside is a different color from outside; you can eat the peel, less garbage Oranges: softer; only orange; juicy sections; you can't eat peel; no stem; can't make sauce or pie with them; grow in warm places; can be messy
End	Both healthy fruit that people enjoy eating that can be turned into juice.

- Tell students that you will be learning and practicing writing comparisons over the next few weeks.

Features of Comparison Writing

Before launching into writing comparisons with your class, it is important to spend time teaching them some of the important features of this form of writing. Over the next few lessons, you will be teaching some key features of comparison writing through a Whole-Class Write comparing cats and dogs.

FEATURE 1: THE VENN PLANNER

- Begin the lesson:

   As all of you know, good writers always plan before they start to write. When writing comparisons, making a plan is likely the most important thing a writer can do. Without a plan, ideas can become very mixed up and then the reader will get very mixed up! Luckily there is a very simple way to make a plan for comparisons.

- Draw a large Venn diagram on the board or interactive whiteboard. Explain that a Venn diagram is the best way for writers to organize their ideas before they write a comparison, because it helps to organize similarities and differences very clearly.
- Write the word *Dog* on one side of the Venn, the word *Cat* on the other, and the word *Both* in the centre. If possible, show images of the animals.
- Ask students to compare these two animals. Remind them that comparing means thinking of how they are the same and how they are different. Give students a few moments to think and then invite them to share their ideas with a partner.
- Begin with similarities and invite students to share their ideas. Record the information in the center of the Venn: e.g., both animals, pets, mammals; both have whiskers, fur, paws, tail.
- Ask students to think of ways dogs and cats are different. Invite them to use this phrase "Dogs …but cats…" Model an example: *Dogs bark but cats meow.*
- As students share their sentences, record ideas on either side of the Venn. Ideas might include the following: dogs need to be walked but cats don't; some

Depending on the grade level, you might choose to introduce the terms "compare" and "contrast" when discussing similarities and differences.

dogs like swimming but cats don't; cats wash themselves but dogs need to be washed; some dogs can be trained to help blind people and police officers but cats can't.

- End the lesson:

> Before writing a comparison, it is very important to make a plan first. Venn diagrams are the best way for writers to organize their thinking before they start to write comparisons. Over the next few days, we are going to learn how to take these ideas from a Venn diagram and write a comparison of cats and dogs.

FEATURE 2: LANGUAGE OF COMPARISON

The language of comparison is key to a successful piece of comparative writing because it helps the writer organize ideas and the reader navigate through the information. Of the languages associated with nonfiction text structures, the language of comparison is likely the most important for students to learn.

- Remind students that, in comparison writing, a writer is telling the reader how two things are the same and how they are different.
- Revisit the Venn diagram and remind students how Venn diagrams help writers organize their ideas for writing a comparison.
- Explain that they are going to learn some special words and phrases that writers use when comparing things.
- Draw an anchor chart on the board or interactive whiteboard, with *Similarities* heading the left column, and *Differences* heading the right.

> Let's start words that can help us talk about similarities. If I want to tell my reader how cats and dogs are the same, what word could I use?

- Model an example: *Cats and dogs **both** have fur.* Record the word *both* on the anchor chart under *Similarities*.
- Ask students if there is another word you could use instead of *both*. Invite students to think of another word and share their cat-and-dog sentence with a partner. Invite students to share and record words on the anchor chart. Statements of similarity could include:

> Cats have fur and dogs do *too*.
> Cats have fur and dogs *also* have fur.
> Cats *as well as* dogs have fur.
> A cat's fur *is the same as* a dog's.

- Continue the lesson:

> Now let's look at differences. If I wanted to tell my reader how dogs and cats are different, what word could I use?

- Model an example: *Dogs bark **but** cats meow.* Record the word *but* on the anchor chart under *Differences*.

> Now, *but* is a good word to use (this might stimulate a few giggles), but if you have too many *but*s in your writing, your reader will start to get bored. Luckily,

there are some excellent *but* replacements that can help your writing sound more interesting!

- Invite students to think of another way to say cats and dogs are different. Depending on the grade level, students might not have been exposed to these particular words, but it is important to include at least four different options for students to use when contrasting. Model some examples and record words on the anchor chart.

> Dogs bark, *however* cats meow.
> Dogs bark *whereas* cats meow.
> Dogs bark *compared to* cats, who meow.
> Dogs bark. *On the other hand*, cats meow.

  Other contrasting words include *while, although, instead, yet, unlike*.
- Write the phrase *-er than* on the board. Explain that *-er than* is a very important way to talk about differences. Ask students if anyone knows what *-er than* means or could make an *-er than* sentence about cats and dogs. Model an example: *Most dogs are bigger **than** cats.*
- Invite students to think of an *-er than* sentence about cats and dogs and share it with a partner. (Most cats are quiet*er than* dogs. Often dogs are friendli*er than* cats. Dogs are easi*er* to train *than* cats.)
- Explain that it's important for writers use words like *most* and *often* because there are always exceptions.
- Students can practice forming contrasting sentences using *more…than*: e.g., Cats are *more* independent *than* dogs. Dogs are *more* active *than* cats.
- End the lesson:

> When we write comparisons, it is very important for writers to use the words that will help their writing be clear for their readers. Some words are useful when writing about how things are the same and other words are useful when writing about how things are different. This anchor chart will be left up in the room so that you can remember these words when you are writing.

COMPARISON WORDS

Similarities	Differences
• *too* • *also* • *both* • *and* • *as well as* • *similar* • *like* • *same as*	• *but* • *although* • *however* • *whereas* • *on the other hand* • *compared to* • *even though* • *while* • *yet* • *-er than* • *more/less than*

Whole-Class Write

Based on the lessons teaching students the structure, plan, and language of comparative writing, students will participate in a guided lesson to complete a whole-class write comparing cats and dogs.

- Begin the lesson:

> So far we have learned the skeleton, plan, and important words that writers use when they are writing a comparison. Today we are going to take what we have learned and work together to write a comparison of cats and dogs.

- Revisit the Venn diagram showing similarities and differences between cats and dogs. Remind them that a Venn is a simple way for writers to get their ideas organized before they write.
- Review the text structure of comparisons: Both–Same–Different–End. Explain that each section of text structure is one drawer that we need to fill. (See lesson on organization on page 43).
- Explain that it is important to clearly introduce both topics at the beginning so that the reader knows what you are comparing. Remind students that it's also important to "hook" your readers with an interesting beginning.

Teacher Model

> *When trying to decide what kind of pet to buy, many people consider cats or dogs. Cats and dogs are popular pets. Some people like cats and some prefer dogs, but both make great companions. You might not think that these animals are anything alike, but they have many things in common as well as a lot of differences.*

- Continue the lesson:

> The next drawer is going to contain information about how cats and dogs are the same. Before I start writing, let's think about all the ways dogs and cats are the same.

- Invite students to work in pairs to finish this sentence:

> Cats and dogs are both _____ (pets, mammals, furry, domestic, either one color or multicolored, cute, cuddly, friendly, loving)

- You could make this into a bit of a game. Partners take turns making a sentence, going back and forth until they run out of ideas. Invite students to share out.
- Model writing:

Teacher Model

> *Cats and dogs have many things in common. Both cats and dogs are mammals. This means are covered in fur, give birth to live babies, and feed their babies milk. They both like to be petted and cared for by their owners. They both add a lot of love to a family and most people think they are both very cute and cuddly.*

- Ask students what they noticed about your writing. (You used the word *both* a lot!) Count up the number of times you wrote the word *both* (four times). Invite students to help you change some of the sentences so that there is a little variety. (Use *also, too, as well*.) Refer to the anchor chart of comparison words on page 127 to help.

- Continue the lesson:

  Now that we have told our reader how cats and dogs are the same, we need to tell them how they are different.

- Invite the students to think of ways that cats and dogs are different in appearance and behavior. Start with appearance and invite students, in pairs, to complete the following sentence:

  Dogs _____ but cats _____. (dogs come in different sizes but most cats are the same size; dogs can have curly hair but most cats have straight hair; dogs can have short or long tails but most cats have long tails)

  Have students take turns thinking of sentences until they can't think of any more.

- Model writing:

Teacher Model

When comparing cats and dogs, you will probably notice a lot of differences in how they look and act. First of all, dogs come in many different shapes and sizes but most adult cats are about the same size. Most cats have fur that is straight but some dogs can have curly hair, shaggy hair, or very short hair. Dogs also have different-sized ears and tails, but cats have mostly long tails and pointy ears that are similar in size. Cats can be striped but dogs can't. As for how they act, dogs and cats are very different. Most dogs are more active than cats and need to be walked and bathed. Some dogs can swim and fetch sticks but cats can't swim or fetch. Cats don't need to be walked and they are more independent than dogs. Dogs can be trained to help people who are blind or can become police dogs but cats can't. Also, dogs chase sqirrels but cats chase mice.

- Ask students what they noticed about the writing. (Too many *but*s!) Invite them to help you "replace your *buts*" by using some of the words from the anchor chart (see page 127). (Use *whereas, however, compared to*.) Remind students that it's important to use the words *some, most,* and *often* because your sentence might not be true of all dogs and cats.
- Remind students that the last part of the text structure of a comparison is where the writer recaps his or her ideas. Ask the students what a recap is. Make connections to a recap of a baseball or hockey game on TV. Explain that the broadcaster shows the important plays one more time and repeats the final score. This is what a writer has to do in the final paragraph: review the important points one more time and explain why it's important to know the differences.

Teacher Model

As you can see, both cats and dogs have many similarites and differences. Both are cute, cuddly mammals and make loyal pets. Cats are more independent and don't need as much care as dogs, but you can train dogs to do tricks. Both cats and dogs make great pets, but knowing how they are different might help you choose to have one or the other—or both!

- End the lesson:

> It is important for writers of comparisons to be organized and clear when sharing the similarities and differences of their two subjects. It's also important for writers to use comparison language so readers don't get confused.

LESSON SUMMARY: ANCHOR CHART

- Review the goals for comparison writing and create an anchor chart for future reference

---

Comparison Writing

- Includes a title
- Clearly states the two subjects at the beginning
- Follows the Both–Same–Different–End structure
- Includes the language of comparison: words for similarities and differences
- Ends with closing statement that summarizes the main points

---

Independent Write

Anchor Books

Julie Cummins, *Country Kid, City Kid* (P, I)   Jenny Sue Kostecki-Shaw, *Same, Same but Different* (P)
Bobbie Katz, *We're Different; We're the Same* (P)

P = primary
I = intermediate
Note that book level is a suggestion only; all books can be used at any level. See page 23.

Based on the preceding lessons, students should be ready to begin writing an independent comparison. For their first independent writing, I prefer to provide students with comparative topics that do not require additional research. Once students become familiar with writing structure and language of comparisons using background knowledge, you can follow up with a writing piece connected to a unit in science or social studies that requires research. Here are suggestions for topics that do not require research; however, some might require background knowledge. Compare

This sample is by a student in Grade 2.

- apples and oranges (see sample at left)
- cats and rabbits
- police officer and fireman
- summer and winter (or any two seasons)
- football and rugby (or any two sports)
- XBox and PlayStation
- book and e-reader
- Harry Potter and Percy Jackson

- private school and public school
- moms and dads
- kids and grownups
- skiing and snowboarding
- going to a movie theatre and watching a movie at home
- being rich and being famous
- being grounded and being in jail

- Once students have selected a topic, pass out the Venn Planner (page 133).
- Allow students time to complete the Venn with similarities in the centre and differences on the sides.

- Comparison Planning Pages for Intermediate and Primary students can be found on pages 133 and 134. These organizers can be used to help your students structure their ideas in more detail after completing their Venn diagrams.
- When students are ready to start writing, remind them of the Both–Same–Different–End structure. Review the Comparison Writing anchor chart (page 130).

Remember that your intent is to describe to your reader similarities and differences between two different subjects. Start by introducing both subjects to your reader. Then write about how they are the same. Next, talk about the differences. Finally, write an ending and mention both topics one final time.

Lesson Extensions

ANIMAL COMPARISONS

Anchor Books

Judy Diehl and David Plumb, *What's the Difference? 10 Animal Look-Alikes* (P, I)

Justin Heimberg, *Who Would Win?* (I)

Isabel Thomas, *Lions Vs. Tigers: Animals Head to Head* (I)

Isabel Thomas, *Shark Vs. Killer Whale: Animals Head to Head* (I)

Isabel Thomas, *Alligator Vs. Crocodile: Animals Head to Head* (I)

P = primary
I = intermediate
Note that book level is a suggestion only; all books can be used at any level. See page 23.

After providing students with an opportunity to practice writing the structure and language features of comparisons with topics that do not require research, students can use their knowledge to do a comparison of similar animals. Explain that they must research information about both animals before writing. The Comparing Animals Planning Page (page 136) can be used when students are gathering facts about their two animals. Possible animal comparisons:

- wasps and bees
- hares and rabbits
- crows and ravens
- butterflies and moths
- porpoises and dolphins
- leopards and cheetahs
- insects and spiders

- turtles and tortoises
- horses and donkeys
- alligators and crocodiles
- toads and frogs
- sharks and whales
- hamsters and gerbils

COMPARATIVE SHOWDOWN!

Deadliest Warrior was a TV series in which historical or modern warriors and their weapons were compared to determine which of them would be victorious if they fought each other, based on tests performed during each episode. Weapons, battle strategies, and battle leaders were compared and, in the end, the deadliest warrior would be revealed. This notion of keeping score is also the format of a nonfiction series by Jerry Pallotta called Who Would Win? These books provide readers with facts and great pictures comparing two similar animals and leave it up to the reader to decide who would win in an animal showdown. These make great models to show students how to write their comparisons in the form of a showdown that invites readers to decide who would win. Using these books as models, students could develop a series of categories in which to compare their subjects and then award points to each side. The winner could be revealed at the end.

Comparison Writing Extensions

Combining Comparison with Persuasion/Opinion

Sometimes, when comparing two topics, a writer also wants to share his/her opinion; i.e., which they think is preferable in some way. To combine these writing styles, students would need to have had lessons on persuasive writing (see Chapter 6) in order to understand how to incorporate their opinion into the comparison.

The most significant difference between a neutral comparison and a persuasive comparison is that the writer must clearly state his/her opinion in the opening paragraph before proceeding to describe the similarities and differences. Voice would also be an added feature, as the writer is adding an opinion to the piece.

Comparing Cultures

Anchor Books: Jeannie Baker, *Mirror;* Stacey Schuett, *Somewhere In the World Right Now*

These books take the reader around the world and show how people live. They could be used as models for students to compare and contrast their lives with others in different places around the world.

Comparing Homes

Anchor Book: Giles Laroche, *If You Lived Here: Houses of the World*

Readers discover the fascinating structures in which people live all around the world. This book would be a perfect anchor for inspiring writing that compares homes.

Venn Planner

Name: _____

Comparing

_____ and _____

Comparison Planning Page: Intermediate

Name: _____

Both _____ and _____

_____

_____

_____

Same: How are _____ and_____ the same?

Examples:

_____

_____

_____

_____

Different: How are _____ and_____ different?

Big Idea:_____(feature)

_____

Examples:

_____

_____

_____

_____

Different: How are_____ and_____ different?

Big Idea:_____(feature)

Examples :

_____

_____

_____

_____

_____

Comparison Planning Page: Primary

Name: _____

	BOTH
	_____
	_____
	_____
	_____
	_____
	_____
	SAME
	_____
	_____
	_____
	_____
	_____
	_____
	_____
	DIFFERENT
	_____
	_____
	_____
	_____
	_____
	_____
	END
	_____
	_____
	_____
	_____
	_____
	_____

Comparing Animals Planning Page

Name: _____

	Animal 1	Animal 2
Description: What does your animal look like? Size? Shape? Color? Fur, feathers, or scales?		
Behavior: What can your animal do? Swim? Run? Fly?		
Habitat: Where does your animal live? Water? Land? Cave? Underground?		
Food: What does your animal eat? Does it hunt?		
Enemies: Which animals hunt or kill your animal?		
Babies/Life Cycle: How does your animal grow? Live birth or eggs? How long does it take to grow up? How long does it live?		
Other Interesting Facts		

8 The Power to Explain

When children are two or three years old, they go through a definitive period in their development in which they begin to wonder about the world around them. For anyone who has experienced this stage with their own children, what starts out as cute curiosity ends up becoming an endless stream of questions that we often don't have answers to. When a three-year-old discovers the word *why*, it can be torturous for parents! Yet the very word *why* indicates that, even at a young age, children are seeking explanations for how the world works.

One of the key reading strategies we teach students is to question the text. Asking questions propels our thinking forward and extends our understanding. The big thinkers of the world are grounded in the wonderings around them; the world around us advances because questions are asked and answers are discovered and explained. Scientific discovery is grounded in these question–answer journeys.

Explaining how or why something works is an important writing structure and the beginning of understanding the cause–effect pattern found in the reading and writing material students will encounter as they move into higher grades. And while this type of writing is usually reserved for older students, it is my belief that we should tap into the natural curiosity that younger children demonstrate and provide them with engagement in this form of writing. As with some of the other less-familiar writing forms, one of the reasons I think teachers don't focus on this form of writing is that we, ourselves, might not feel confident in the structure and language. We stick with description because we are familiar with the form. But, as Tony Stead so wisely points out, if we focus only on story writing and descriptive report writing, we are limiting our students' writing demonstrations, expectations, and engagements.

While some of the other text structures included in this book can be completed without research, this particular form requires some investigation and fact-gathering. Focusing initially on a whole-class write is a good way for students to learn the purpose, structure, and language for this writing form. For the purpose of these lessons, we will be exploring scientific explanation.

> Children need time and opportunity for immersion, demonstrations, and engagements in scientific explanations if they are to become proficient writers in these forms. (Tony Stead, 2002: 155)

Overview of Explanatory Writing

Purpose

- To explain *how* or *why* something happens

Text Structure: How/Why–Because–Because–So There!

1. **How/Why:** Identify or define what is being explained
2. **Because:** Explanation of the *how* or *why* (cause–effect elements)
3. **Because:** Further explanation, including facts in a logical sequence
4. **So There!:** Concluding or summarizing statement

Language Features

- Linking words: *then, next, finally, after, then, before*
- Explanation words and phrases: *because, that is the reason, that is because, that's what happens when, that is why, due to, because of, then, if, why, and*
- Nonfiction Features: diagrams, labels.

Examples

P = primary
I = intermediate
Note that book level is a suggestion only; all books can be used at any level. See page 23.

Scientific Explanations How

- How do rainbows form?
- How do leaves change color?
- How did the dinosaurs die?
- How do stars form?
- How do lungs work?
- How do glaciers form?
- How do volcanoes erupt?
- How does a hurricane form?
- How birds fly
- How planes fly

Scientific Explanation Why

- Why does it snow?
- Why does it rain?
- Why do windows fog up?
- Why do turtles have shells?
- Why do some things float and some sink?
- Why do I burp?
- Why do snakes shed their skin?
- Why does ice melt?
- Why does the moon change shape?

Scientific Explanation Anchor Books

I Wonder Why? series, Kingfisher (P, I)
Melvin Berger, *Why I Sneeze, Shiver, Hiccup and Yawn* (I)
Franklyn Branley, *What Makes Day and Night?* (P, I)
Anna Claybourne, *Head-to-Toe Body Questions* (Crabtree Connections series) (I)
Anna Claybourne, *Tadpole Story* (P)
Rudyard Kipling, *Just So Stories* (P, I)
Betsy Maestro, *How Do Apples Grow?* (Let's Read and Find Out About Science series) (P)
Betsy Maestro, *Why Do Leaves Change Color* (Let's Read and Find Out About Science series) (P)

Christopher Niemann, *That's How!* (P)
Peter Neumeyer, *Why We Have Day and Night?* (P)
Jenny Offill, *11 Experiments That Failed* (I)
Brigitte Raab, *Where Does Pepper Come From? And Other Fun Facts* (P, I)
Catherine Ripley, *Why? The Best Ever Question and Answer Series* (P, I)
Amy Shields, *National Geographic Little Kids First Big Book of Why* (P, I)
Mark Teague, *How I Spent My Summer Vacation* (I)

Intent

The intent of scientific explanation is to describe and clarify to the reader *how* something works or was formed, or *why* something happens or is the way it is. These explanations are often connected to scientific phenomena or happenings in nature in relation to science.

Form

Explanatory writing generally begins with the writer identifying what is going to be explained in the form of a heading or an opening statement. The writer then explains the *how* or *why* components in logical sequence, often including cause–effect statements. There is a usually a concluding or summarizing statement to end.

The rhyme pattern developed to help students remember the form of explanation sounds like this: How/Why–Because–Because–So There!:

1. *How/Why:* statement of how something happens or is the way it is
2. *Because:* reason 1 (why or how it happens)
3. *Because:* reason 2 (why or how it happens)
4. *So There!:* conclusion

Language Features

The following are features commonly found in explanatory writing:

- Linking or transition words: *first, then, next, finally*
- Explanation words and phrases: *because, that is the reason, that is because, that's what happens when, that is why, due to, because of, then, if, why, and*
- Nonfiction features: often labeled diagrams support the explanation
- Subject-specfic vocabulary and terms

Writing Techniques

This form of nonfiction writing tends to be more factual, limiting some of the writing techniques that are used to enhance other forms. The following are mini-lessons that could be introduced or reviewed during your focus on this form:

- Nonfiction Text Features (see lesson on page 36)
- Interesting Details (see lesson on page 37)
- Organization (see lesson on page 43)

Links to Content Areas

Science is grounded in questions and explanations. There are hundreds of ways to link this form of writing to your science content, either as a whole-class investigation or as individual writing. Students can select from a variety of questions generated either by them or by you. Below are some examples of writing topics related to science content:

Weather	• How tornadoes (hurricanes, tidal waves) form • How it snows (rains) • Why the wind blows • How rainbows (clouds) form • Where lightning (thunder) comes from
Human Body	• Why we need water (food) • How we digest food • How the heart (digestive system, respitory system) works • Why I blink (yawn, burp)
Geography	• How the Grand Canyon formed • How earthquakes happen • How waves form • Where rivers (lakes) come from • Why volcanoes errupt
Plants	• How plants grow • Why leaves change color • Why plants grow toward the light • Why some trees lose their leaves
Force and Motion	• How gravity works • Why a car rolls down a ramp • How airplanes fly • How a simple machine (ramp, pulley, etc.) works
Matter	• How ice melts • Why some things float and some sink • Why water freezes
Electricity	• Where electricity comes from • How a lightbulb works • How a flashlight lights • Why the power sometimes goes out
Light	• Where light comes from • How light can travel at different speeds
Earth and Space	• Why we have seasons • How the moon changes shape • Why stars shine at night • Where the moon goes in the daytime • Why it is hot on Mercury
Animals/Insects	• How animals become extinct • How insects can walk on the ceiling without falling off • Why the dinosaurs disappeared • Why snakes shed their skins • Where insects go in winter • How frogs grow • How birds fly • How spiders spin webs • How fish breathe

Assessment

This rubric can be used as a benchmark for assessing your students' comparison writing pieces. As always, I encourage you to make adjustments to the any of the comments to meet the needs of your specfic grade.

EXPLANATORY WRITING ASSESSMENT RU

NY = Not Yet Meeting expectations
M = Meeting expectations (minimal level)
FM = Fully Meeting expectations
Ex = Exceeding expectations

Title:	NY	M	FM	Ex
Form: Begins with a clear statement highlighting what is going to be explained and ends with a concluding statement.				
Organization: Follows the text structure for explanation of How/Why–Because–Because–So there!; includes relevant information in a logical order.				
Research: Student is able to locate information from books and nonbook sources.				
Writing: Engages the reader with interesting details, words, and voice.				
Style: Includes explaining words and phrases.				
Visuals: Includes diagrams and labels that support the explanation.				
Mechanics: Writing demonstrates effective use of spelling, punctuation, and grammar.				
***Wow!* Factor:** Writing shares information in a particularly interesting, unique, or surprising way.				

Introduction to Scientific Explanation

Anchor Texts

I Wonder Why? series, Kingfisher (P, I)
Jennifer Berne, *On a Beam of Light: A Story of Albert Einstein* (P, I)
Highlights Kids Science Questions: http://www.highlightskids.com/science-questions/archives
Tana Hoban, *I Wonder* (P)

Catherine Ripley, *Why? The Best Ever Question and Answer Book about Nature, Science and the World around You* (P, I)
Catherine Ripley, *How? The Most Awesome Question and Answer Book about Nature, Animals, People, Places and You!* (P, I)

Catherine Ripley's *How?* and *Why?* books are excellent models of scientific explanations and are among my favorites for stimulating students to wonder about the world around them.

• Using the anchor book *On a Beam of Light*, begin the lesson:

This morning I am going to read you a story about a very famous scientist named Albert Einstein. Albert Einstein spent his life asking questions and trying to exlain how and why things happen.

- After reading the story, discuss how Albert Einstein would not have discovered all that he did if he hadn't first started by asking questions. Tell students, "Good readers ask questions while they read; good thinkers ask questions all the time!"
- Take your students on a *wonder walk* around the school or neighborhood. Pass out the My Wonder Walk template (page 147) and, if possible, provide each student with a clipboard and pencil.
- Explain how sometimes you can go for a walk and not really notice things. But today you want the students to be like Albert Einstein and wonder while they walk. Invite students to record their *wonderings* on the clipboard. Encourage students to focus on questions that start with either *how* or *why* (see sample at left).
- Model some of your own wonder questions:

  Why are some clouds fluffy and some fill the sky? How do leaves change color? Why do leaves fall but needles don't? Why is moss only growing here and not there?

- After the walk, invite students to record on the bottom of the page any other questions they might have about the world.
- Gather for discussion. Write *I Wonder Why…* on the top of a chart paper, the board, or the interactive whiteboard.
- Ask students to share some of the questions from their wonder walk with a partner. Invite students to share out and record some of their questions on the chart.
- Ask if there were other things they were wondering about the world that they also recorded: e.g., Why did the dinosaurs die? How do spiders spin webs?
- Tell students that when a writer is answering a *how* or *why* question connected to science, the writer is giving a *scientific explanation*. Explain that writing explanations in science helps readers by telling them how or why something happens.
- Invite students to chose one question they think they might know the answer to and be able to explain. Have them record their answer on the bottom of the page. These initial explantations that students write can be viewed as their baseline understanding of explanatory writing.

Structure and Features of Scientific Explanation

- Copy the following on a chart stand or interactive whiteboard:

  Why does it snow? Because it gets cold and falls from the sky.

  Ask students if they think that is a good explanation for why it snows. (We hope they will agree its not a good explanation!) Ask them why it is not a good explanation. (Because it doesn't really explain how, but just gives facts about snow; it's confusing because the reader doesn't know what "it" is referring to.)
- Remind students that every text form has an inner skeleton or structure, and that it's important for a writer to understand and follow the structure when writing. Introduce the text structure for writing explanations: How/Why–Because–Because–So There! Record the headings on the board:

This sample is by a student in Grade 3.

How/Why: the *how* or *why* question

Because–Because: details to explain the *how* or *why* in a logical sequence

So There!: ending or summarizing statement

There are many series on a wide variety of topics that use the question–answer format to explain the world's *hows* and *whys*. Your school or local library will likely have enough copies for pairs of students to read.

- Explain that, when writing scientific explanations, it is important to gather facts to include in their writing. Tell them that they will be looking through some books to see how other writers explain how or why things happen.
- Provide students (in partners or individually) with an opportunity to explore some *How* and *Why* books.

Language of Scientific Explanation

- As students read the anchor books, ask them to look for special words that the writer uses to explain things.
- After students have spent time exploring these books, gather together to discuss what they noticed. Ask students if they noticed any special words that the writers used when they were explaining. Make an anchor chart:

Explaining Words

- because
- after
- when
- then
- and
- if
- that is why/this is why
- that is because/this is because
- that's what happens when

- End the lesson:

  When a writer is explaining how or why something happens, it is called an explanation. When you are writing a explanation, you need to follow the skeleton Why?/How?–Because–Because–So There! You also need to use some special explaining words so that your writing is easier for your reader to follow.

Whole-Class Write

Anchor Books: Erin Edison, *Snow*; Cassie Mayer, *Snow*; Marion Dane Bauer, *Snow*

In this lesson, teacher and students will be working together to create a whole-class explanation for how it snows.

- Begin the lesson:

  Last time, we learned about a new form of writing called *explanation*. Today we are going to write an explanation together.

It's helpful to have a few books that include facts to help you with your explanation.

- Write *How Does it Snow?* at the top of a chart paper or on the interactive whiteboard. Ask students how this question could be turned into a statement that will help the reader know exactly what is about to be explained. (How it snows)

Explain that often a writer will start with a question asking what they want to explain, but that they turn the question into a statement to help their reader.
- Read aloud from one of the anchor books and invite students to listen for important information about how it snows.
- Record some of the facts that you gathered:

  - Snow is frozen rain.
  - Puddles form on the ground when it rains.
  - The sun comes out and the puddles turn into steam.
  - Steam goes up into the air and makes clouds.
  - When the clouds get too full, they let the water out.
  - Water comes out of the clouds as rain.
  - If the temperature outside is below freezing, the rain freezes and it turns into snow.

- Explain to students that you are now going to turn your facts into an explanation using the How?/Why?–Because–Because–So There! structure.
- Remind students that it's very important to begin by stating what it is you are about to explain, otherwise your reader will be confused.
- Model how to add a begining and ending to the explanation to make the writing interesting for the reader. Encourage students to refer to the anchor chart of Explaining Words (see page 143). Invite students to help you as you write. Remind students that explanation titles are often in the form of a statement that answers a *how* or *why* question.

Teacher Model

How It Snows

Have you ever wondered why it snows? Here's how!

__When__ it rains, it makes puddles on the ground. __Then__ the sun comes out and the puddles go into the air like steam. The steam mixes with dust and makes clouds in the sky. __After__ more rain and more puddles and more steam, the clouds get very big and full. __When__ the clouds gets too full to hold all the water, they have to let the water out. __That is why__ it rains. If the temperature in the air is very cold, __then__ the water will turn into snow.

And __that is how__ it snows! Isn't that "cool"?!

- Discuss the features and language they noticed in your writing. Highlight or underline the explaining words and phrases.
- Ask students for examples of how you tried to make the writing interesting. (humorous ending)
- Ask students to help you add diagrams with labels to show the different stages.

Review the important parts of an explanation and create an anchor chart:

Explanation Writing

- Has a beginning that tells you what will be explained
- Has reasons for why or how something happens
- Is written in an order that makes sense
- Uses linking words like *first*, *next*, *then*, and *finally*
- Uses explaining words like *because*, *so*, *therefore*
- Ends with a closing statement
- Includes pictures or labeled diagrams

Independent Write

After the whole-class write, students should be able to write their own explanation from a question they would like to explore. Key to this writing is access to texts at your students' reading level; you can guide their questions according to the books you have access to.

- Pass back students' initial My Wonder Walk pages and ask them to read the question and explanation they wrote at the bottom.
- Ask what they think of the explanations they wrote and how they might be able to make them better. (adding more information and facts; using explaining words; using sequence words; adding labeled diagrams)
- Tell students they will be rewriting their explanations to try to improve on them. Or students can chose to explore a different question.
- Pass out Gathering Facts for Explaining template (page 148). Remind students that they are to record facts on this page, but do not need to write in complete sentences until later in the writing process.
- Provide students with several periods to explore their topic. If students are struggling to find information, they might need your guidance to help them choose a different question to explore.
- When students have finished gathering information, review the anchor charts on pages 143 and 145 to remind them of the important aspects of explanation writing and the language of explanation.
- Reread the How it Snows piece (page 144) to the class. Remind students that their writing needs to begin with the how or why question and an interesting opening statement that is revisited in the closing statement.
- Review some of the explaining words students will likely need to include in their writing. Invite students to be thinking about diagrams they might add to their writing to help their readers understand the ideas and facts.
- Students will likely need several periods to complete their writing and diagrams.

One of the challenges in this piece of writing will likely be supporting students in their search for information that is at an appropriate reading level, as some of the material connected to these topics tend to be at a high level. I do recommend the I Wonder Why books by Kingfisher or Catherine Ripley's *Why?* and *How?* books, as they provide clear, simple explanations for many of the topics students will be wanting to explore.

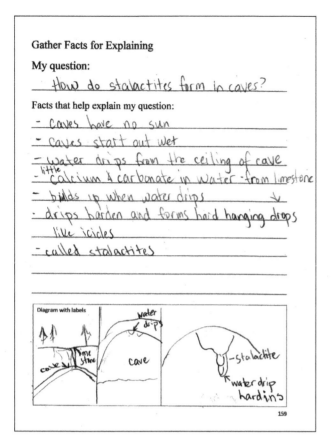

Gather Facts for Explaining

My question:

How do stalactites form in caves?

Facts that help explain my question:

- caves have no sun
- caves start out wet
- water drips from the ceiling of cave
- little Calcium & carbonate in water from limestone
- builds up when water drips
- drips harden and forms hard hanging drops like icicles
- called stalactites

Diagram with labels

cave stone / time stone / water drips / cave / stalactite / water drip hardins

159

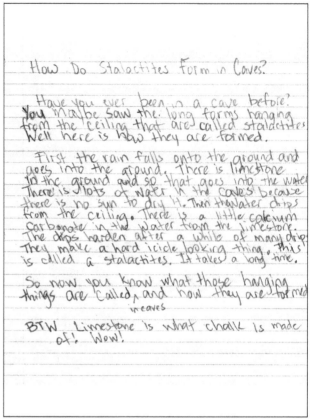

How Do Stalactites Form in Caves?

Have you ever been in a cave before? You maybe saw the long forms hanging from the ceiling that are called stalactites. Well here is how they are formed.

First the rain falls onto the ground and goes into the ground. There is limestone in the ground and so that goes into the water. There is lots of water in the caves because there is no sun to dry it. Then the water drips from the ceiling. There is a little calcium carbonate in the water from the limestone. The drips harden after a while of many drips. They make a hard icicle looking thing, this is called a stalactites. It takes a long time.

So now you know what those hanging things are called, and how they are formed in caves.

BTW Limestone is what chalk is made of! Wow!

These samples are by a student in Grade 6.

- It is worthwhile, once the students have completed their investigations, to have them compare the new writing to their initial pieces. Students will be surprised at how much growth their writing shows and how much they have learned about writing scientific explanations.

My Wonder Walk

Name: _____

Wonder Walk Questions:

_____
_____
_____
_____
_____
_____

Other Questions:

_____
_____
_____
_____
_____
_____

Choose one of your questions you think you can answer. Write it here:

_____
_____
_____
_____
_____

Explain your answer here:

_____
_____
_____
_____
_____
_____

Gathering Facts for Explaining

Name: _____

My question:

_____
_____
_____

Turn your question into a statement:

_____
_____
_____

Facts that help explain what happens:

_____
_____
_____
_____
_____
_____
_____
_____
_____
_____

Diagram with labels

9 The Power to Report

One of the most interesting forms of nonfiction writing is the nonfiction narrative—the stories left behind by people and events of the past preserved in print. We have an undeniable curiosity about the lives of fascinating people and events that make up the tapestry of our past. Nonfiction narratives retell or recount specific events of our world and the lives of people in it. They tell the true tales of ordinary people who become extraordinary through their actions, or accounts of events and occurences that affect the world. Nonfiction narratives often follow the beginning–middle–end of a fictional narrative because, in most cases, facts are presented in a sequential manner. This form of writing can easily be connected to content areas and the topics lend themselves well to multi-genre writing.

For the pupose of this section, there are specific lessons on the three main areas of nonfiction narrative: biography, history, and current events.

Overview of Narrative Nonfiction

NARRATIVE NONFICTION AT A GLANCE

Purpose
- To retell, recount, and highlight specific events and facts about the life of a particular person for the purpose of informing and entertaining
- To give a chronological account of important events
- To highlight a person's or people's contribution to the world

Text Structure: Who/What–What–Where–When–How–Wow!
1. **Who/What:** full name of subject; event(s)
2. **What:** description of accomplishments, jobs, hobbies, hopes and dreams/ description of event(s)
3. **Where:** birthplace, where subject went to school, lived, traveled/where event(s) took place
4. **When:** dates of birth, death; years subject attended school; accomplishments in chronological order/date(s) of event or events
5: **How:** the subject's impact on the world/the importance of the event(s)
6. **Wow!:** interesting facts to wow your reader

Language Features
- Specifies participant or subject
- Uses simple past tense (*was, did, went, had*)
- Action verbs (*climbed, saw, discovered, sailed; happened*)
- Linking words dealing with time (*first, after, later, then, before*)
- Details to add interest
- Nonfiction Features: diagrams, labels, pictures and/or photographs, timelines

Examples
- Biographies of family members, friends, sports stars, movie stars, inventors, politicians, world leaders, authors, etc.
- Retellings of past events in history: e.g., building of a railway; sinking of the Titanic; Hurricane Katrina; the origin of Halloween, Christmas or other religious celebrations
- News reports of current events in the world

P = primary
I = intermediate
Note that book level is a suggestion only; all books can be used at any level. See page 23.

Nonfiction Narrative Anchor Books

BIOGRAPHY

Series

Capstone Paperback, First Biographies series (P)

Grosset and Dunlap, Who Was/Is… series (I)

Kathleen Krull, The Lives of… and What the Neighbors Thought series (I)

Children's Press, Rookie Biographies series (P)

Scholastic Canada, Biographies: includes Canadian inventors, explorers, heroes, pioneers, leaders, artists, and stars (I)

Smart About Art series: includes Frida Kahlo, Vincent Van Gogh, Pablo Picasso, Claude Monet, etc. (P, I)

Time for Kids series: includes Willam B. Rice, *Jane Goodall* (P, I)

Individual Titles

Amelia Earhart: Flight Around the World (A Short Biography for Children) (P, I)

Gene Barretta, *Neo Leo: The Ageless Ideas of Leonardo Da Vinci* (P, I)

Gene Barretta, *Timeless Thomas: How Thomas Edison Changed Our Lives* (P, I)

Jennifer Berne, *Manfish: The Story of Jacques Cousteau* (P, I)

Jennifer Berne, *On a Beam of Light: A Story of Albert Einstein* (P, I)

Don Brown, *One Giant Leap: The Story of Neil Armstrong* (P, I)

Don Brown, *A Wizard from the Start: The Incredible Boyhood and Amazing Inventions of Thomas Edison* (P, I)

Jacqueline Davies, *The Boy Who Drew Birds: A Story of John James Audubon* (P, I)

Amy Ehrlich, *Rachel: The Story of Rachel Carson* (P, I)

Deloris Jordan, *Salt in His Shoes: Michael Jordan in Pursuit of a Dream* (P, I)

Kathleen Krull, *Wilma Unlimited: How Wilma Rudolph Became the World's Fastest Woman* (P, I)

Kathleen Krull, *The Boy on Fairfield Street: How Ted Geisel Grew Up To Become Dr. Seuss* (P, I)

Kathleen Krull, *The Boy Who Invented TV: The Story of Philo Farsnworth* (P, I)

Laurie Lawlor, *Rachel Carson and Her Book That Changed the World* (P, I)

Doreen Rappaport, *Martin's Big Words: The Life of Dr. Martin Luther King, Jr.* (P, I)

Maxine Trottier, *Terry Fox: A Story of Hope* (P, I)

Jeanette Winter, *The Watcher: Jane Goodall's Life with the Chimps* (P, I)

Jeanette Winter, *My Name Is Georgia* (P, I)

HISTORICAL EVENTS

Nikki Giovanni, *Rosa* (P, I)

Ellen Levine, *Henry's Freedom Box: A True Story from the Underground Railroad* (P, I)

Pam Munoz Ryan, *Amelia and Eleanor Go for a Ride* (P, I)

Pam Munoz Ryan, *When Marian Sang: The True Recital of Marian Anderson* (P, I)

Bettye Stroud, *The Patchwork Path: A Quilt Map to Freedom* (P, I)

Carole Boston Weatherford, *Freedom on the Menu: The Greensboro Sit-Ins* (P, I)

Jeanette Winter, *Follow the Drinking Gourd* (P, I)

Intent

The intent of nonfiction narrative is to retell or recount specific events in a person's life or in a current or past event. The purpose is to inform and entertain, with more emphasis on facts and less on subjective comments. The events are often organized and described in sequential order.

Form

Nonfiction narratives usually begin with a title that includes some indication of the person or event. This is followed by details that provide some background information and/or a setting to help orient the reader. The narrative continues with a series of events, usually presented in chronological order. Sometimes the writer includes personal observations or comments. The piece often ends with an evaluative comment that reflects the writer's feelings about the impact, significance, or importance of the person or event.

The rhyme pattern developed to help students remember the form of nonfiction narrative sounds like this: Who/What–What–Where–When–How–Wow!

1. *Who* your subject is/*What* the event is
2. *What* happened? (this could be a series of events)
3. *Where* the event(s) occurred
4. *When* the event(s) occurred
5. *How* this person or event affected the world
6. *Wow!*: amazing or interesting facts to wow your reader

Language Features

The following language features are commonly used in nonfiction narratives:

- Specifies participant or subject
- Uses simple past tense: *was, did, went, had*
- Action verbs: e.g., *climbed, saw, discovered, sailed; happened*
- Linking words dealing with time: *first, after, later, then, before*
- Interesting details to add interest
- Nonfiction text features: diagrams, labels, pictures and/or photographs; time-lines

Writing Techniques

Nonfiction narrative lends itself well to many of the writing technique lessons. These techniques enhance both the style and the form of the writing, enabling the writer to engage the reader in a more interesting and effective way. The following are writing techniques that can be introduced as mini-lessons during your focus on this writing form:

- Nonfiction Text Features (see lesson on page 36)
- Introductions to Hook Your Reader (see lesson on page 42)
- Interesting Details (see lesson on page 37)
- Organization (see lesson on page 43)
- Triple-Scoop Words (see lesson on page 38)

Links to the Content Areas

Writing biographies linked to your science or social studies topics is an effective way for students to practice writing nonfiction narratives as well as to learn about the people and events that have had an impact on our world and society. Below are some suggestions of biography links to content areas:

Science	Social Studies
Biography of famous scientist, famous architect, famous inventor	• Family: biography of a family member • Explorers: biography of a famous explorer • People: biography of an athlete, celebrity • Government: biography of a famous political leader • Ancient Civilizations: biography of an ancient warrior, political figure, citizen • First Nations: biography of an Aboriginal leader • Arts: biography of a famous author or artist

Assessment

Here is an assessment rubric you can use when evaluating your students' narrative nonfiction writing pieces. These should be used to give your students feedback for their writing as well as provide you with a way of tracking trends in your class which may guide your instruction.

NARRATIVE NONFICTION WRITING ASSESSMENT RUBRIC

NY = Not Yet Meeting expectations
M = Meeting expectations (minimal level)
FM = Fully Meeting expectations
Ex = Exceeding expectations

Title:	NY	M	FM	Ex
Form: Includes who, what, where, when, how; explains how the person or event had an impact on the world (positive or negative).				
Organization: Follows the text structure for narrative nonfiction; includes clear headings, chronological events.				
Writing: Engages the reader with interesting details, words, and voice.				
Visuals and **Text Features:** enhance the information and are complete and clear; timeline is complete, accurate, and neat.				
Mechanics: Writing demonstrates effective use of spelling, punctuation, and grammar.				
***Wow!* Factor:** Includes information to wow the reader.				

Introduction to Nonfiction Narrative

Visit the library and stock up on a wide variety of biographies to leave in your classroom library. Try to schedule daily read-alouds of short excerpts from these collections so that students become familiar with the purpose and text structure of a biography.

- Explain to students that they will be learning a new form of nonfiction writing called *nonfiction narrative*. Explain that *narrative* is another word for story, and that *nonfiction* means it is true or real. Ask students if they can think of an example of a true story. (the true story of someone's life; the true story of a real event that happened in the past; a newspaper story)
- Explain that sometimes writers choose a real person or real event that they want to tell their reader about. Before writing the story, the writer must try to find out everything he/she can about the topic. Then the writer takes the information and writes it a little bit like a fiction story, with a beginning, middle, and end. Only this time, the people and events are true, not made up.
- Continue the lesson:

    When writing about a real person or a real event, writers often use a different writing style.

    Pass out copies of the Sample Biographies on page 166, showing two pieces of writing about Canadian scientist David Suzuki. Explain that both examples are about the same person but that they are written in different ways.
- After reading, ask students what they noticed the writer included in each of the examples. Have them discuss in partners.
    (Sample 1 included description that focused on the person's appearance and personality. Sample 2 included facts—where he was born, dates, family, job, etc.)
- Explain that when a writer's intent is to describe someone, things like appearance, personality, and feelings would be important. But when a writer's intent is to tell the story of someone's life, they need to include important facts, as in Sample 2.
- Explain that the proper name for a piece of writing about another person's life is *biography*.

    Biographies are ususally written about a famous person who is either alive or has already died. A biography is a type of nonfiction narrative because the writer is telling the story of a person's life. When a writer is telling the story of his or her own life, it is called an *autobiography*.

- Ask students what important information might be included in a biography. (name, nationality, date of birth, family, school, job, etc.)
- Explain that the skeleton of a nonfiction narrative sounds like this: Who–What–Where–When–How–Wow!
- Invite students to help you create an anchor chart by adding details to this skeleton:

    Who?—the full name of subject and subject's family
    What?—description of accomplishments, jobs, hopes and dreams

Where?—birthplace, where subject lived, went to school, traveled

When?—date of birth, death; when subject attended school; accomplishments in chronological order

How?—the subject's impact on the world

Wow!—interesting facts to wow the reader

Tell students that, over the next few weeks, they will be learning how to write an autobiography and a biography.

Whole-Class Write: Teacher Biography

Interactive Plan

- Remind students that nonfiction narrative is a form of writing that tells the story either of someone's life or of a past or current event. Explain that they will be working together as a class to write a biography about you, their teacher.

  Now, before a writer can write a biography, what do you think they need to do? (research and ask questions to find out everything they can about the person) What happens if the person you are writing about has either died or is living somewhere else and you can't talk to them? (read information about them) Today, our subject is going to be me, so you will be able to ask me questions in person.

- Ask students what a writer's intent is when writing a biography? (to tell my reader all about a person) What questions could we ask our subject if we want to find out about them? (Remember the Who–What–When–How–Wow! structure.)
- Pass out biography books to pairs of students. Give them time to look through the books to find out the following:

  - What important information did the writer include about the person?
  - How did writer organize the ideas?

- Gather class together to discuss their findings.
- Using yourself as a model, ask students what important things might need to be included in a biography about you:

  Biography of _____
  - Introduction
  - Where and when she/he was born
  - Her/his family
  - Her/his school days as a child
  - Her/his school days as a teacher
  - Hobbies/Interests/Talents
  - Accomplisments
  - Her/his hopes and dreams

- Explain that now the plan for the biography is in place, the next step is to gather the information. Organize the class into eight groups and explain that each group will be responsible for gathering information for one section of the biography. Try to ensure that there is a capable student in each group who will record the information for the group.

- Explain that students will be acting like reporters, and each group will need to come up with three or four questions on their topic to ask.
- Write the following questions on the board:

  - Do you like cats?
  - What is your favorite pet?
  - Do you have a pet? Tell me about it.

Ask students which question would provide the most important information for a biography and why. (third question, because it is very specific to the person) Explain that questions with *yes* and *no* answers often don't provide a lot of information.

- Provide students with time to generate questions pertaining to their topic that will give them the most information.
- After students have finished writing their questions, begin the interviews. Take turns having students interview you. These interviews could either be in front of the class or in small groups while the other students are working.

Interactive Draft

- Begin the lesson:

  Yesterday, your groups wrote questions and interviewed me. Today you are going to use the information you recorded to write a paragraph.

- Set a goal of four to five sentences to record the information. Remind students to try to present the information in an interesting way.
- Explain that the topic of their paragraph must be clearly identified in the first sentence. Example: *Ms. Gear has many interesting **hobbies** she enjoys doing.*
- Review writing goals (see the My Writing Goals anchor chart on page 34):

  How do you make writing interesting for a readers? (voice, similes, triple-scoop words, visuals)
  How do you make sure your reader is not confused? (spelling, punctuation, spacing)

- Allow time for groups of students to work together to write the paragraph. Likely each group will choose one recorder who will write the sentences while others contribute ideas.
- When each group has completed their section, they can present it to the class. Use this opportunity to highlight groups that have created an interesting and engaging paragraph.

Independent Write

Classmate Biography

After working through the whole-class biography, students will be ready to develop an individual biography. In this lesson, students will begin to learn the process of gathering information about another person in the class through asking a series of interview questions and then using the information to write a biography of their classmate.

- Write down the names of each class member, including yourself, on strips of paper; fold them and put them into a hat or box.
- Begin the lesson:

   Last week, we wrote a whole-class biography about me. This week you will be writing a biography about a classmate.

- Ask students what things might be important to include in the biography. Record their ideas on an anchor chart:

   What to Include in a Biography
   - Full name of the person
   - Date and place of birth
   - Family
   - School
   - Favorite things
   - Hobbies/Talents
   - Accomplishments/Awards
   - Hopes and dreams

- Pair up students by pulling names by two out of the hat. Or you might decide to let students choose their own partners.
- Explain that, for the next few lessons, students will need to spend time working to collect information about their partner and to record this information. Remind students that they will need to to ask their partner questions, just like they had asked you questions for the whole-class biography.
- Pass out copies of the Biography Planner: Classmate on page 167. Go over the interview questions they intend to ask and model how they don't need to write complete sentences on the Planner, as long as they record the key information.
- Provide several periods for students to interview their partners and record the information. Circulate the room and while they working and provide extra support for those students who may need it.

WRITING

- Once students have completed their interviews and recorded information, review the key elements of a biography. Record these on an anchor chart.

A good biography
- includes an interesting opening
- states the person's full name
- follows the Who–What–Where–When–How–Wow! structure
- is written in third person (*he/she*, not *I*)
- includes interesting facts and information
- has clear sections with headings
- includes visuals, if possible
- is neat; uses correct spelling and punctuation

For younger students, the writing of the biography can be broken down into one section at a time, so they don't get overwhelmed. A Grade 2/3 class I was working with worked on one section per week.

- Provide blank books for students to write their biographies in—three or four legal-sized pages folded in half and stapled. Explain that each new page can be used for a section and that each section should have a heading.
- Remind students that one of our goals as writers is to make sure our writing is interesting. Write the following introductory sentences on the board:

    1. *This is a biography of Olivia Sloan. Now I'm going to tell you about her.*
    2. *So you'd like to hear about the interesting life of Olivia Sloan? Well, she is quite an amazing person!*

Read them aloud. Ask students which sentence is a more interesting introduction to a biography and why. (Second sentence is more interesting because it asks a question and has voice.) Remind students that biographies should be written in third person; i.e., should not have the word "I" in them.

Autobiography

Jamie Lee Curtis's *A Brave Book of Firsts* and *When I Was Little: A Four-Year-Old's Memoir of Her Youth* are both excellent anchor books for this lesson.

Students can use their background knowledge of the structure and language of a biography to write an autobiography.

PLANNING

- Remind students that a biography is an account of someone's life written by someone else. Write the word *autobiography* on the board and ask students what they think it might mean? Give them a hint: *auto* means "self." Explain that an autobiography is the story of a person's life, told by him/herself.

    Last week, we wrote biographies about someone else. This week we will be writing about ourselves. Writing an autobiography is easy in one way and difficult in another: easy because we know ourselves better than anyone else; but difficult because we know so many things that have happened to us, it's hard to know what to include and what to leave out. One of the ways a writer can figure out what events to write about is to make a timeline. A timeline can help you plan out the important events in the order they happened.

I like to refer to the key events as "chapters" in your life story.

- Explain that, before making the timeline, they first need to think about some of the important events in their life that they would want to include. Brainstorm possible important events: birth, first day of school, moving to a new house, birth of sibling, first pet, accident or hospital visit, losing a tooth or getting braces, special holiday or family event, award or big win in sports/school play/performance.
- Tell students to think about 12 events that they feel are imporant to their life story and list them on the Timeline Planning Page (page 168). Provide time for students to list their events. Encourage students to ask for help from home if they are not sure about a specific date.
- Once students have completed their list, model how to plot the events on a timeline. Model on chart paper or the interactive whiteboard using a timeline format. Students can use Timeline: Primary (page 169) or Timeline: Intermediate (page 170) to plot their events.

This sample is by a student in Grade 7.

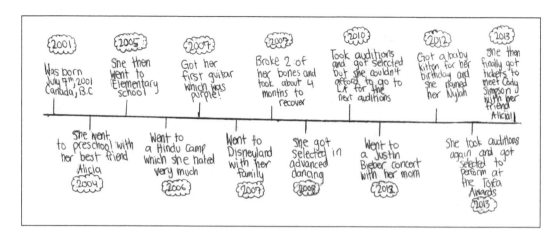

WRITING

- Using the same format as they used for writing the biography of a classmate (Biography Planner: Classmate on page 167) students can begin to record their own information for their autobiography. Because no interviewing is required, and since they have already gone through the process, many will be able to complete this page independently. Use this time to support students who require additional support.
- Once students have completed the page, review the anchor chart on what makes an interesting biography (see page 156).
- Younger students can write their autobiography in either a small-book format or on a single sheet with a drawing or photograph. Older students can use a poster format to display their information.
- Encourage students include visuals and text features to support their information. Additional visuals might include:

  - timeline (see lesson on page 157)
  - self-portrait
  - additional photos of the student's early childhood
  - symbols or pictures to represent hobbies, interests
  - map of where student was born
  - social media profile page
  - flags representing student's family origin
  - fact box; i.e., *Did you know...?*
  - a tag cloud (e.g., Wordle) of key words about the student

Dave Biln, a Grade 6 teacher at my school, does a large biography project with his class every June. He begins with having the students write a personal timeline and autobiography, and then a timeline and biography about a famous person. The students create double-sided posters to present their information.

Whole-Class Write: Biography of a Famous Person

After you have scaffolded students' understanding of the structure and language of a biography, they are ready to move into a more research-based piece about a famous person. In this lesson, the students will work with you and create a whole-class biography of Jane Goodall.

Erin Edison, *Jane Goodall* (P, I)
Patrick McDonnell, *Me...Jane* (P, I)
Jim Ottaviani, *Primates: The Fearless Science of Jane Goodall, Dian Fossey, and Biruté Galdikas* (P, I)

Jeanette Winter, *The Watcher: Jane Goodall's Life with the Chimps* (P, I)

P = primary
I = intermediate

I have chosen Jane Goodall for this lesson because I have always been fascinated by her life story and because I own several good biographies about her. You can choose another person for this lesson, but try to choose someone not too familiar to your students, preferably a person with an accompanying biography. See options on page 150.

- Write the word *famous* on the board or interactive whiteboard. Ask students what it means. (well-known, recognized by many, somebody who has done something important)
- Ask what makes a person famous. (accomplishments; did really well in something, like acting, singing, sports, art; discovered something; invented something or explored somewhere; leader of a country; did something very bad, like a crime, war)
- Ask students to think about a famous person they know or admire. Have them share ideas with a partner.
- Have students brainstorm in partners what things they would like to know about a famous person. (where they were born, family, school, what they did, what impact they had on the world) Remind students that the *How* part of a biography is very important. The writer needs to include how this person has affected the world and the difference he/she has made.
- Remind students that a piece of writing about another person is called a biography. Write the name *Jane Goodall* on the board. Ask students to tell what they know about this person, based on the name. (likely only that she is female, and perhaps that she is "good")
- If possible, show a photo of Jane Goodall with chimpanzees. Ask students to look at the picture and tell what they know from the picture.
- Explain that Jane Goodall is a scientist who is famous for her research on chimpanzees. Read aloud the story "The Watcher" and encourage students to listen for important information about Jane Goodall's life. Older students can record facts on paper or on the Biography Planner: Famous Person (page 171). Younger students could be assigned to listen for facts under one of the following headings:

> **Who:** name of person and family members
> **What** did this person do? (job, accomplishments)
> **Where:** birthplace
> **When:** date of birth and death
> **What** did this person do to make him/her famous?
> **How** did this person influence the world?
> **Wow!:** additional interesting facts

- After students have listened and recorded information about Jane Goodall, invite them to turn and discuss with a partner what they have learned about her.
- Explain that, now that they have gathered information, they can begin to write. Depending on the grade level, small groups could be responsible for different sections, as outlined on pages 154–155.
- Review the anchor chart on page 156 for what makes an interesting biography.

- Ask students to help you with an opening sentence for a biography about Jane Goodall that will draw readers in and make them interested in reading. Use books on Jane Goodall as models for opening sentences. Review opening sentences that "hook" the reader (page 42).
- Write the following examples on a chart or the interactive whiteboard:

  1. *Today I'm going to tell you about a scientist named Jane Goodall.*
  2. *You have probably heard of black apes and brown apes, but have you ever heard of a "white ape"? Well, that is the nickname given to British scientist Jane Goodall, who has lived with and studied chimpanzees in Africa almost her whole life, because some people think she is part ape!*

  Discuss which one is more interesting and why. (second one, because it includes an interesting fact and a question, and engages the reader)
- Depending on how much time you want to spend on this class piece, you can have each group tell you two or three facts per heading while you scribe on a whiteboard or interactive whiteboard.
- As an alternative, break the class into small groups and assign each group one section to write. Encourage students to work together cooperatively and to be respectful of everyone's ideas. When groups are finished, invite them to share their writing with the class. Sections can be combined into a class book about Jane Goodall. Each group could provide a visual or nonfiction feature to accompany their paragraph.

Independent Write

Biography of a Famous Person

There are some outstanding biographies that can be used as models for this non-fiction form. Having a collection of these anchor books in your classroom and sharing them with your students will expose them to interesting life stories and examples of excellent writing. See biography list on page 150.

There are many Top 100 lists of famous people avaliable on the Internet. Dave Biln, Grade 6 teacher at my school, shows his students *100 Most Inflential People in History* videos (produced by TIME magazine) over several days. The students then make their top three choices for who they would like to write about.

- Begin the lesson:

  We have been learning about writing biographies. We worked on a class biography of Jane Goodall last week. This week, you will be chosing your own famous person to write about.

- Students can choose from a wide range of famous people to focus on, including leaders, scientists, explorers, actors, artists, singers. This could be a good opportunity to link writing to a science or social studies topic you are focusing on; see chart on page 152. You can let students choose their subject or assign them someone to write about.
- Continue the lesson:

Include a lesson or review on accurately recording resources as an important aspect of research.

  Before writing a biography about a famous person, we need to gather facts about his or her life by reading other books about this person. Your job in the next few lessons is to search for facts about your famous person. You will need to gather this information in note form.

- Pass out copies of the Famous Person Fact Find sheet on page 172. Explain that there are headings at the top to guide students with their research, but that they can change the headings if they wish. Explain that the notes will be collected and included in their assessment.
- Depending on the grade you teach, you might want to spend some time reviewing note-taking. Remind students that, when we research, it is important that we write down key facts, but not entire sentences. Invite students to help you record notes under the appropriate headings. Model using the following sentence:

> *A short time after his sister Maria was born in 1891, the Einstein family went to Munich where Albert first attended elementary school and subsequently Luitpold grammar school. He was an "average" pupil but was already showing an interest in science and mathematics.*

Teacher Model

Family/Early Life
- younger sister Maria
- 1891 moved to Munich

School
- went to elementary school at Luitpold Grammar School
- average student
- early interest in science and math

- Provide several periods for students to research their famous person, using books from the library and the Internet. Encourage them to record their notes on the Fact Find sheet and to keep track of the books and websites they have used.
- Suggested websites that include collections of biographies, written for kids:

  http://gardenofpraise.com/leaders.htm
  http://mrnussbaum.com/bio2/
  http://www.ducksters.com/biography/

- Once students have completed their Fact Find sheets and you have had a quick check that they have enough information, they will be ready to write their biogaphy. Review the elements of a good biography on the anchor chart (page 156); review the author's intent (page 153).

Lesson Extensions

PRESENTING

In addition to having students present information in writing, you might encourage students to include visuals and nonfiction features to highlight and share the information: additional lessons might be requried. You might choose to use this opportunity to introduce and incorporate different writing forms for a more extensive multi-genre project. Other writing forms include

- timeline
- map of birthplace
- flag of birth country
- portrait or self-portrait (hand-drawn, not computer-generated)

- visuals or symbols to represent hobbies, interests, accomplishments
- obituary (see lesson on page 161)
- How to Be... poem (see lesson on page 78)
- persuasive piece on why this person is the most famous (see Chapter 6)
- letter in first-person from the famous person to someone else
- journal or diary entry in the voice of famous person
- social media profile of the person
- birth certificate
- Facebook page

WRITING AN OBITUARY

Anchor Books

Hugh Montgomery, *The Daily Telegraph Book of Obituaries* (I)

Harry Quetteville, *Thinker, Failure, Soldier, Jailer: An Anthology of Great Lives in 365 Days – The Telegraph* (I)

Marvin Siegel, *The Last Word: The New York Times Book of Obituaries and Farewells: A Celebration of Unusual Lives* (I)

P = primary
I = intermediate

An obituary is a unique form of writing. The obituary writer must capture essential information about a person's life and present it in a clear, concise format. This no-frills style of writing is a useful exercise in highlighting only the most important facts while respectfully acknowledging a person's life. Once students have researched and become familiar with a famous person, they should have enough background knowledge to be able to write a competent obituary.

- Begin the lesson:

  We have been spending a lot of time gathering information about famous people for our biographies. Some of your famous people are still alive and some of them are no longer living.

- Explain that an obituary is a notice of death that is published in a newspaper or online. It lets people know that a person has died and often includes a brief biography.
- Pass out copies of sample obituaries and ask students to read them with a partner. While they are reading, ask them to keep track of the things they notice about the writing and what is included.
- Project a sample obituary on the overhead or document camera and do a read-aloud/think aloud, pointing out the key elements: full name, age at death, family members, occupation, character traits, what he/she was known for. Continue reading through and noting that the ending usually includes information about the funeral or memorial services and donations.
- Invite students to help you write an obituary for a character in a book:

Teacher Model

POTTER, Harry
July 31, 1980–August 27, 2013
Harry Potter, skilled wizard of Hogwarts School of Witchcraft and Wizardry, died unexpectedly during a sword battle with archenemy Lord Voldemort. Predeceased by his parents James and Lily Potter. He leaves behind beloved wife Ginny Weasley and his

three children—James Sirius, Albus Severus, and Lily Luna—uncle Vernon Dursley, aunt Petunia Dursley, and cousin Dudley, along with many friends from Hogwarts, including Ron Weasley and Hermione Granger. Harry was born in England and attended Hogwarts School of Witchcraft and Wizardry. He was a valued member of Gryffindor House and star player on the Gryffindor Quidditch team. Harry often risked his life to protect those he loved and will be remembered for his bravery and courage. Funeral service to be held at Hogwarts School of Witchcraft and Wizardry on Saturday, September 3rd at 2 pm.

- Explain to students that they are going to be writing an obituary for their famous person. Remind them of the importance of recording the dates accurately. Explain that if their famous person is still alive, they are to pretend that he or she has died. In this case, they will need to make up the date and cause of death.
- Review important words and phrases associated with obituaries: *passed away, survived by, leaves behind, pre-deceased by, will be remembered for.*
- Students can use the Obituary template on page 173.

ICE (Interesting Current Events) Report

Writing and presenting a report on a current event is a common exercise in many elementary schools and is an an excellent way to combine reading, writing, and speaking skills in one activity. Often students are asked to locate an interesting article from the newspaper, to read it, and to write a summary of key events. Sometimes an oral presentation is included. This type of report writing is considered a form of nonfiction narrative because it is a retelling of a true story and uses a structure similar to that of a biography. In this lesson, we revisit the Who/What–What–Where–When–How–Wow! skeleton with a focus on an event, rather than on a person's life.

- Choose a current event story from the local newspaper to use as a model. If possible, choose an event that students will be familiar with. Prepare to project as a scan using a document camera, or on an overhead transparency. Pre-read so you have a general idea of the content.

Because I like to focus on the origin of words, I like to connect the word *report* with *reporter*.

- Begin the lesson:

  For the past few weeks we have been learning to retell the story of a person's life. This type of writing is called *nonfiction narrative*. This week we are going to learn another kind of nonfiction narrative called a *report*. A report is a retelling of a true event that has either just happened or happened in the past. If it is something that just happened, we call it a *current event*. We are going to learn to write an ICE, Interesting Current Event, report.

The reading level of newspapers that students are assigned to read is often too high. Providing students with material at their reading level encourages succcess. *What in the World?* is an interactive current-events resource that provides teachers with classroom sets of newspapers with a reading level accessible to elementary students. Files are also avaliable in PDF format for easy interactive whiteboard application: see http://www.lesplan.com/en/subscriber-issues

- Explain that a report follows the same text structure or skeleton as a biography. Review the Who/What–What–Where–When–How–Wow! structure.
- Ask students what the author's intent would be when writing a report. (to share the facts of the event in the order they happened)
- Project the newspaper article and model a read-aloud/think-aloud. Invite students to help you locate the *who, what, where, when, how,* and *wow* facts.
- Use a transparency or projection of the ICE Report template (page 174) and model how to complete it.

- Using the information you recorded, model how to write a summary of the article. Remind students that your intent is to provide your reader with a clear account of what happened in the correct order.
- Explain to students that it is important to clearly state as much information at the beginning so that the reader knows what the event is, then follow up with more details. You don't want your reader to be confused!
- Pass out copies of the ICE Report template (page 174) for students to use.

Lesson Extension: APE (Amazing Past Events) Report

Anchor Texts

Nicholas Brasch, *Natural Disasters* (I)
Stephen Currie, *Man Made Disasters* (I)
Ned Halley, *The World of Disasters* (I)
Mary Ann Hoffman, *Hurricane Katrina* (I)
Tamara Leigh Hollingsworth, *Unforgettable Natural Disasters* (I)
Kirby Lawson, *The Two Bobbies: A True Story of Hurricane Katrina, Friendship, and Survival* (P, I)

Barbara Barbieri McGrath, *The Storm* (P)
Cormac O'Brien, *The Daily Disaster: Read Life Stories of 30 Amazing Disasters* (I)
Cormac O'Brien, *The BP Oil Spill* (Scholastic A True Book series: includes the Hindenburg, the Titanic, Exxon-Valdez spill, Krakatoa, nuclear meltdowns) (I)
Stewart Ross, *The Great Fire of London* (I)
Rene Schmidt, *Canadian Disasters: 43 True Stories* (I)

WEBSITES

http://science.discovery.com/life-earth-science/10-natural-disasters.htm
http://listverse.com/2007/09/07/top-10-deadliest-natural-disasters/

http://www.disasterium.com/10-worst-natural-disasters-of-all-time/

P = primary
I = intermediate

Using the same format as in the preceding lesson on current events (page 163), students can investigate true events of the past. Focusing on disasters, both natural and man-made, proves to be a captivating topic for most intermediate students. By reading aloud about these historic events and immersing students in books that describe them, you can pique their interest and reinforce the structure of report writing.

Students can work in pairs to complete the APE Report template on page 175, choosing to report on either a man-made or natural disaster. It is helpful to distinguish the difference between the two and brainstorm examples of each (see chart below). Completed reports can be shared with the class by posting them in a sequential timeline around the room and/or by collecting them and making a class book. Encourage students to include visuals and nonfiction text features in their reports.

Natural Disasters	Man-Made Disasters
• Black Death • Potato Famine • Eruption of Pompeii • Eruption of Krakatoa • African Famine • 2004 Boxing Day Tsunami in Asia • Hurricane Katrina • Hurricane Sandy • 2011 Earthquake and Tsunami in Japan	• Sinking of the Titanic • Explosion of the Hindenburg • Space Shuttle Explosion • Nuclear Power Plant Explosion in Chernobyl, Russia • BP Oil Spill • Exxon-Valdez Oil Spill • Fukushima Nuclear Disaster

Sample Biographies

Sample 1

David Suzuki is a Canadian scientist. He has gray hair the color of a rain cloud and eyes that sparkle like black diamonds. He is very friendly and his laugh sounds like a river. David Suzuki is as smart as a calculator. His dream is that one day our Earth and oceans will be free of pollution and that people and nature will live together in harmony.

Sample 2

David Suzuki is a Canadian scientist and award-winning writer and environmentalist. He was born in Vancouver, British Columbia, in 1936 to parents of Japanese descent. David Suzuki cares a lot about the environment and works hard to educate people about how to protect and care for nature. He was the host of a popular TV show called *The Nature of Things* and has written more than 30 books for children and adults about nature and environment. Before he retired in 1971, he was a professor of genetics at the University of British Columbia.

Biography Planner: Classmate

Name: _____

Full name _____
Place of birth _____
Date of birth _____
Family/Cultural Heritage _____ _____ _____
School (name of school, grade, favorite subject, teachers) _____ _____ _____
Hobbies/Interests/Favorite things _____ _____ _____
Wow! Facts (achievements, trips, awards, skills) _____ _____ _____
Hopes and Dreams _____ _____ _____

Timeline Planning Page

Name: _____

Event	Date

Timeline: Primary

Name: _____

Timeline of _____

Timeline: Intermediate

Name: _____

Time Line of _____

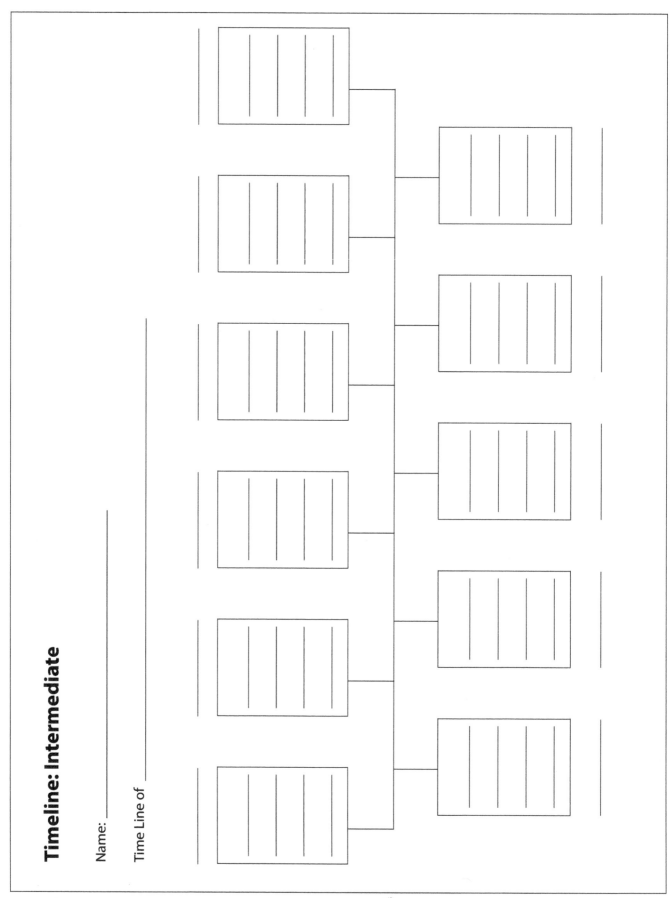

Biography Planner: Famous Person

Name: _____

Full name _____
Place of birth _____
Date of birth _____ Date of death (if person has died) _____
Famous for _____
Family _____ _____ _____
Early Life/Childhood/School _____ _____ _____
Interests/Hobbies _____ _____ _____
Accomplishments/Achievements _____ _____ _____
Wow! Facts _____ _____ _____

Famous Person Fact Find

Name: _____

Biography of _____

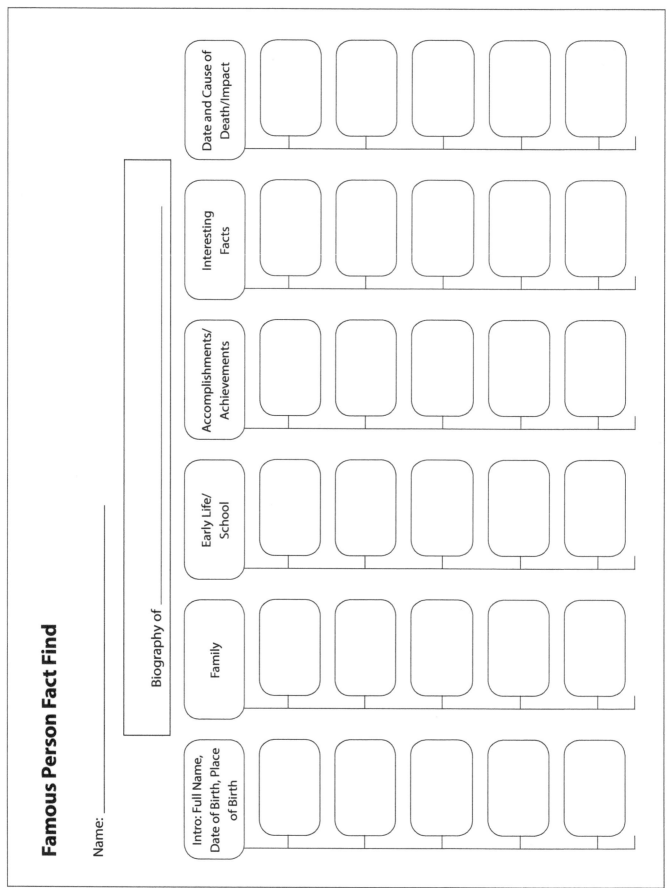

Intro: Full Name, Date of Birth, Place of Birth

Family

Early Life/ School

Accomplishments/ Achievements

Interesting Facts

Date and Cause of Death/Impact

Obituary

Name: _____

Last name: _____ First name(s): _____

Date of birth: _____ Date of death: _____ (if unknown, make it up!)

Cause of death: _____ (if unknown, make it up!)

Pre-deceased by _____

Education: _____

Achievements: _____

_____

Will be remembered for

_____

_____

Funeral Services (when, where)

_____

_____
_____
_____
_____
_____
_____
_____
_____
_____

ICE Report

Name: _____

Headline: _____

Source: _____

Type: ☐ Local   ☐ Provincial   ☐ National   ☐ International

WHO/WHAT: person(s) involved in event/event

_____

WHERE: location(s) of event _____

WHEN: date of event _____

WHAT: sequential summary of events; use transition words: *first, next, then, after,* etc.

_____
_____
_____
_____
_____
_____
_____
_____
_____

HOW this event is important

_____
_____
_____

WOW!: interesting details

_____
_____
_____

APE Report

Name: _____

Headline: _____

Event: _____

Type: ☐ Natural   ☐ Man-made

WHO/WHAT: person(s) involved in event/event

_____

WHERE: location(s) of event _____

WHEN: date of event _____

WHAT: sequential summary of events; use transition words: *first, next, then, after,* etc.

_____
_____
_____
_____
_____
_____
_____
_____

HOW this event is important

_____
_____
_____

WOW!: interesting details

_____
_____
_____

Final Thoughts

Writing is powerful. Nonfiction writing is essential. One of the ways we can prepare our students for success in the real world is to help them become more proficient and engaging writers. To communicate information, to provide instructions, to voice an opinion, to motivate and inspire others—these are the real reasons people write. It is up to us to move our students beyond the factual report writing we grew up with into other forms of nonfiction writing.

As I come to the end of this book, I reflect on my audience and my intent. My audience: teachers—teachers like me, who believe in their craft, who believe in their students, and who believe that they have the power to make a difference. Teachers like me, who reflect and rejoice every day because teaching is transforming, exhilarating, and valuable.

My intent in writing this book is to inspire, to encourage, and to support. My intent is that, after reading this book, you will feel inspired to teach your children to be active writers of informational texts; that you are encouraged to make nonfiction writing an enjoyable and attainable experience for all students; and that you now have the support to guide your students through practical lessons into a variety of nonfiction writing forms.

I am grateful to have an opportunity to teach amazing students every week and then be able to share my experiences with other teachers. And so I give my thanks to you, my reader, for inviting me into your classroom, your school, your professional learning community, your conversations, and your thinking. Thank-you for being a curious, caring teacher who believes that learning is an experience not solely for your students but also for yourself. Thank-you for believing that, through your intentional and purposeful teaching, your students will be better writers in June than they were in September. And finally, thank-you for allowing my learning to be a part of yours.

Acknowledgments

For more than half my life, I have been a teacher. It's the first professional job I ever had and the only one I have ever known. I can honestly say that when I'm standing in front of a group of students eager to learn along with me, it's hard to refer to it as *work*. I am grateful to be able to do what a love at J.W. Sexsmith Elementary School in Vancouver, Canada. There, two days a week, I am surrounded by amazing educators and exceptional students. My students bring me such joy: laughing and learning along with me; sharing their stories; trying their best; and reminding me every day why I became a teacher. They continue to teach me far more than I could ever teach them. I work alongside my colleagues (whom I consider my friends), collaborating on units of study, trying out lessons, sharing favorite books, engaging in conversations, making mistakes, and laughing a lot. This book would not have been completed without their support and collaboration. My sincere thanks to Jacquie Hall, Kimberly Matterson, Duncan Kay, Dani Conrad, Dave Biln, Sarah Liljefors, John Herbert, Amber Leeper, Mary Cottrell, Jeanette Mumford, Jeanette Owen, Sarah Hummerston, Leslie Martin, Leslie Wolrich, Margo McGarry, Wendy Hugli, Sarika Nanda, Carole Murray, Jan Overall, Liz Raagner, Cheryl Davison, Gail Rovere, Andrew Coelho, Tania MacIntyre, and the amazing support team.

A special thank-you to Dave Biln and his amazing Grade 6 class of 2012/2013. They applauded whenever I walked into their class, laughed at my jokes, and demonstrated a keen enthusiasm for anything and everything to do with writing. It was a joy working with them.

Everyone needs a Cheryl—a friend for life. I am forever grateful to my Cheryl, Cheryl Burian, for her generosity and kindness in helping me jumpstart this book. Thank-you for being my "boarding sound," for the sacrifices you made to help me get in the zone, and for being firm about that pedicure. Thank-you for your unconditional friendship and for being the kind of teacher we all aspire to be.

I am blessed to have a circle of loyal friends who love and support me in all aspects of my life, both professionally and personally. Thank-you to Sue Stevenson, Kimberly Matterson, Donna Boardman, Laura Grills, Jen Daerendinger, Kathy Keeler, Katie McCormack, Amy Wou, Krista Forbes, and Meredyth Kezar. Thank-you to my two sisters, Alison Gear and Janet Gear, both extraordinary educators and writers, who are the roots of my family. I am grateful for their unwavering belief in me.

To Carrie Gelson, exceptional educator, blogger, children's advocate, and my kindred spirit in all things related to picture books and teaching: thank-you for your support in de-fogging my blog and supporting my journey. You continue to be an inspiration to me, as you are to so many.

To the members of my book club—Heather, Cheryl, Laura B., Laura G., Krista, Stella, Anna, Melanie, Maria, Bonnie, and Jarma: I so look forward to our monthly gatherings, where I am surrounded by great women, great wine, great books, and great conversations.

When I told Phyllis Simon, co-owner of Vancouver Kidsbooks, that I was working on a new book, I'm not sure if she wanted to jump for joy or run for the hills! But I know that she, store managers Leslie Buffam (Kitsilano), Maggie Blondeau (Surrey), Susan McGuigan (Edgemont), and the amazing staff at all three stores will continue to support teachers, students, libraries, and schools by providing them with the best of the best in children's literature.

I extend my enormous gratitude to Nadia Fortune, Elizabeth Graves, and the rest of the amazing staff at United Library Services for their ongoing support of Reading and Writing Power in schools across BC and Alberta. They generously invite me to "fill my shopping cart" and pretend not to notice when I sniff the new books whenever I visit the warehouse.

I am grateful to Mary Macchiusi, president of Pembroke Publishers, for never pressuring me, always encouraging me, and always believing in my ability to finish this book; and to Kat, my gifted editor, for always taking the time to ask the right questions and guide me to find the answers.

My father, William Irvine Gear, was passionate about words, about literature, about teaching, about life. My mother, Sheila Gear, was a storyteller, a writer, a wise and gentle soul. Together, they have given me an abundance of priceless gifts. I hope they would be proud to see how I am using them.

A special thank you to the Primary teachers from the Delta School District who attended my Nonfiction Writing Power workshops last year, which were made possible through the Barbara Jarvis Foundation, founded by Ab Singh, and co-chaired by Sue Pudek and Catherine Watson. Many attending this debut series last year eagerly took the ideas back to their classrooms, tried some of the lessons, and brought back student samples to share—some of which are in this book. My thanks to Lynda Tyler, Marjan Oghabi, Juanita Hewitt, Ellen Martin, Shelley Davidson, Alison Monk, Louise Shwarz, Cathy Warnock, and anyone I might have missed.

Though my name is on the cover of this book, a great many people have contributed to its development. For acknowledgments in my previous three books, I have gone to great lengths in an attempt to include every single person with whom I have connected through my work as a consultant and workshop presenter. I'm afraid that, after more than ten years of providing in-services and workshops in Canada, the US, and the UK, that list has become too long. So rather than attempting to name individuals, I am offering up a collective thank-you to each and every one of you. Reading and Writing Power continue to develop and thrive in classrooms and schools around the country. It is thrilling for me to see the excitement teachers have when I show a new picture book or share a new lesson at a workshop. It is the greatest compliment I could receive when teachers come up to show me something they have done to change a lesson to make it better for their students or to share a new picture book they are using for one of the strategies. I continue to meet extraordinary teachers, administrators, teacher librarians, support teachers, teacher leaders, literacy coaches, district staff, and parents, all of whom are working together toward one common goal—to make learning better for children. I am inspired by the desire of the many educators who want nothing more than to learn deeply in order to better their craft. It is a privilege to witness these paradigm shifts, big and small, everywhere I go. I do what I do because of you. Thank-you.

When you spend more than a year with a book inside your head, it tends to fill up the spaces in your brain where everyday things usually live. This occurrence is noted most by the people I spend the most time with—my family. To you, I am forever and always indebted because of all the times this book got in the way of my thinking, resulting in (to name a few) lost keys, wrong hockey rinks, burned dinners, and conversations gone astray. Richard, Spencer, and Oliver—I am my best self when I am with you and I thank you for being the three people who fill up the most important spaces in my heart.

Professional Resources

Calkins, Lucy (1986) *The Art of Teaching Writing* (new edition). Portsmouth, NH: Heinemann.

Calkins, Lucy (2003) *The Units of Study for Primary Writing: A Yearlong Curriculum Series.* Portsmouth, NH: Heinemann.

Calkins, Lucy & Sarah Picard Taylor (2008) *A Quick Guide to Teaching Persuasive Writing.* Portsmouth, NH: Heinemann.

Calkins, Lucy & Marika Paez Wiesen (2012) *A Quick Guide to Teaching Informational Writing, Grade 2.* Portsmouth, NH: Heinemann.

Crowhurst, Marion (1993) *Writing in the Middle Years.* Toronto, ON: Pippin Publishing.

Culham, Ruth (2002) *The 6+1 Traits of Writing.* New York, NY: Scholastic.

DiPrince, Dawn (2011) *Twisting Arms: Teaching Students to Write to Persuade.* Austin, TX: Prufrock Press.

Donohue, Lisa (2009) *The Write Beginning.* Markham, ON: Pembroke.

Dorfman, Lynne R. & Rose Cappelli (2009) *Nonfiction Mentor Texts – Teaching Informational Writing Through Children's Literature, K-8.* Portland, ME: Stenhouse.

Duke, Nell, K. & V. Susan Bennett-Armistead (2003) *Reading & Writing Informational Text in the Primary Grades.* New York, NY: Scholastic.

Dymock, Sue & Tom Nicholson (2007) *Teaching Text Structures: A Key to Nonfiction Reading Success.* New York, NY: Scholastic.

Fletcher, Ralph & Joanne Portalupi (2001) *Nonfiction Craft Lessons.* Portland, ME: Stenhouse.

Gallagher, Kelly (2011) *Write Like This: Teaching Real-World Writing Through Modeling and Mentor Texts.* Portland, ME: Stenhouse.

Gear, Adrienne (2008) *Nonfiction Reading Power: Teaching Students How to Think While They Read All Kinds of Information.* Markham, ON: Pembroke.

Gear, Adrienne (2011) *Writing Power: Teaching Writing to Engage Thinking.* Markham, ON: Pembroke.

Graves, Donald H. (1994) *A Fresh Look at Writing.* Portsmouth, NH: Heinemann.

Graves, Donald H. (1989) *Investigate Nonfiction.* Portsmouth. NH: Heinemann.

Graves, Donald H. (1983) *Writing: Teachers & Children at Work.* Portsmouth, NH: Heinemann.

Harvey, Stephanie (1998) *Nonfiction Matters: Reading, Writing, and Research in Grades 3–8.* Portland, ME: Stenhouse.

Heard, Georgia (2009) *A Place for Wonder.* Portland, ME: Stenhouse.

Hoyt, Linda (2002) *Make It Real: Strategies for Success with Informational Texts.* Portsmouth, NH: Heinemann.

Lane, Barry & Gretchen Bernabei (2001) *Why We Must Run with Scissors.* Shoreham, VT: Discover Writing Press.

Lane, Barry (2003) *51 Wacky We-Search Reports: Face the Facts with Fun.* Shoreham: VT: Discover Writing Press.

Loewen, Nancy (2010) *Writer's Toolbox.* Mankato, MN: Picture Windows Books.

McGregor, Tanny (2013) *Genre Connections: Lessons to Launch Literacy and Nonfiction Texts.* Portsmouth, NH: Heinemann.

Meyer, B.J.F. & G. E Rice (1981) "The structure of text" in P.D. Pearson, R. Barr, M.L.Kamil, & P. Mosenthal (Eds.), *Handbook of Reading Research* (319–351). New York, NY: Longman.

Meyer, B.J.F. (1975) *The Organization of Prose and Its Effects on Memory.* Amsterdam: NorthHolland Publishing.

Newkirk,Tom (1989) *More Than Stories: The Range of Children's Writing.* Portsmouth, NH: Heinemann.

Pearson, P.D. & M.C. Gallagher (1983) "The instruction of reading comprehension" *Contemporary Educational Psychology*, 8, 317–344.

Pearson, P. D. & L. G. Fielding (1991) "Comprehension Instruction" in *Handbook of Reading Research: Vol. II*, R. Barr, M. Kamil, P. Mosenthal, and P. D. Pearson (Eds). New York, NY: Longman.

Ray, Katie Wood (1999) *Wondrous Words: Writers and Writing in the Elementary Classroom.* Urbana, IL: NCTE.

Robb, Laura (2004) *Nonfiction Writing From the Inside Out.* New York, NY: Scholastic.

Rog, Lori Jamison & Paul Kropp (2004) *The Write Genre.* Markham, ON: Pembroke.

Routman, Regie (2005) *Writing Essentials: Raising Expectations and Results While Simplifying Teaching.* Portsmouth, NH: Heinemann.

Stead, Tony (2002) *Is That A Fact? Teaching Nonfiction Writing K–3.* Portland, ME: Stenhouse.

Wells, Jan & Janine Reid (2004) *Writing Anchors.* Markham, ON: Pembroke.
Index

Index